Following the Martins

A STORY OF BRINGING HOPE IN PERU, ZAMBIA AND UGANDA

ALLEN SACKMANN

◆ FriesenPress

Suite 300 - 990 Fort St
Victoria, BC, V8V 3K2
Canada

www.friesenpress.com

ISBN
978-1-4602-8456-8 (Hardcover)
978-1-4602-8457-5 (Paperback)
978-1-4602-8458-2 (eBook)

1. SOCIAL SCIENCE, PHILANTHROPY & CHARITY

Distributed to the trade by The Ingram Book Company

Table of Contents

This book is dedicated to the countless couples and small groups who, without fanfare, are committed to improving the lot of others both at home and abroad as their personal mission.

Tom Martin *Cheryl Martin*

Tom and Cheryl Martin:(Photo Courtesy of Helping Cope Through Hope)

Hajara was seven when she was given to a relative to serve as a house girl. That happens a lot in the slums around Mityana, little children — mostly girls — hauling water, scavenging firewood, and cleaning the hovel-like home, all while keeping a watchful eye on still younger children.

She didn't go to school. Her daily labours earned her beatings most days. Being slow. Careless with the little kids. The mistress was cranky. The master was away, or maybe drunk. Life went on, day after dreary day.

In the Ugandan slums, possessions are few, tattered, and often dirty. There is not much to treasure. Pretty much the only thing that can't be stolen or broken is a name. So names are important, often Biblical, as an expression of hope in a place filled with hopelessness. Her name, Hajara, is commonplace; it is derived from Hagar, one of Abraham's two wives, who was the mother of Ishmael, and is a revered woman in the Islamic faith.

Introduction

The Hajaras in the world of the Martins are legion — children abused, neglected and unprotected. Many are simply abandoned. My wife and I were introduced to the plight of such children by Tom and Cheryl Martin when we joined their network of about 350 supporters. This had never been my plan. In fact, our connection to the Martins began mostly out of curiosity.

They were on a mission, that much I knew, when they came to our local church. The presentation was so casual, so unobtrusive, that it didn't seem like one at all. What missionary shows up in cargo pants, a sweat shirt, and a baseball cap to make an appeal for funds, but doesn't actually ask for money? Tom just talked about children, their education, their families, their health — children like Hajara.

Poking around, I found that friends, neighbours and a couple of churches gave them money, and the Martins took the cash afar to spend on school fees, medicine, bedding, shelters. No apparent work plan, no selection process for aid, just a desire to help. The father of one family, whose children were in school courtesy of the Martins, died in hospital miles from home. His body would not be returned home for burial unless someone coughed up about sixty dollars for transport, an amount well beyond the family's ability.

"So we paid," Tom told our church group. That pragmatic approach, where all donations ended up with people in need, was enticing as it seemed unorthodox.

No glitz, no slick organization, no discernible or systematic fund-raising campaigns. Just a next-door couple — a retired school teacher and a retired nurse — whose main mission was to give children a glimpse at what education can do for them and, just as important, instilling the hope that they really could have a brighter future. Spilling over from that mission were the connected needs of adults and families.

One thing always leads to another: helping to alleviate hunger, providing medicine, housing, and, sometimes providing hope through starting micro businesses.

The Martins were certainly different from my skeptical perception of many aid efforts, including those church-based. Charitable donations were something I did because they were something you had to do, especially in response to major disasters or wars, so my benign interest was awakened when I learned how the Martins worked. They were independent, unaligned with any organization, although they worked in harmony with some. There was no costly overhead or organizational hierarchy. Their faith was not displayed on billboards, but in all they did.

They summer at home in Canada. In late fall each year, they head south like many retirees, but not to enjoy the sun. They go to give a leg up to people in Peru, Zambia, and Uganda, until spring, when their own family beckons them back north again. So far, they seemed not too unlike many other retired couples with a sense of duty to make the world a better place. But probing deeper, I began to discover their uniqueness.

Their odd, three-country "mission field," where more than 99 percent of their donations end up helping people in need, was compelling. They emphasize that they are simply a channel, linking stay-at-home people with children and families they'd get to know by name, often leading to bonds so strong that many. supporters accompany the Martins to these countries to cement a lasting relationship. Just as intriguing was the cumbersome name, which explains both their approach and goal: Helping Cope Through Hope (HCTH). "Cope" and "Hope" are the key words which are explained as "Helping Children, Orphans,

*P*risoners and the Poor cope through *H*ealing, Orphanages, *P*rovisions, and Education." Not a name that rolls off the tip of the tongue. The name seemed to cover a waterfront of missionary-type endeavours. A couple in Portugal run a soup kitchen three days a week, feeding about one hundred people at a sitting. A dentist and his wife spend holidays each year in Honduras, providing free dental services. A young American has made clean water his mission. Another couple had the money and compulsion to save migrants on the high seas. The list is extensive and impressive. In many cases, these individuals go without fanfare, but often with some organizational support behind them — a church, a club, or professional organization. The Martins fly solo with the wind under their wings provided by a tiny band of individuals who share a common determination to help desperate people break the bonds of poverty.

New York reporters, Nicholas D. Kristo and Sheryl WuDunn, explain in their book, *A Path Appears*, that hopelessness is the biggest contributor to poverty. For the Martins, that understanding was instinctive rather than the result of sociological research. "But be warned," a *New York Times* reviewer wrote in October, 2014, that "if you want to carry on with your life just as it is, best give [*A Path Appears*] a miss." The same might be said about being caught up in the Martins' world.

My wife and I were already curious through casual conversations before we even laid eyes on the Martins. Meeting and listening to them was both enticing and bewildering. And, as I dug deeper, I learned about the unusual concept that caught the imagination of their North American supporters. Their work was not the "manna-from-heaven" of blowing into town and making a grand impact. No, they burrowed into the very lives of those they touched. The bonds were real, almost familial. They knew each child's name, birth date, and family progress. They read their report cards. They fretted when their charges got sick or disappeared — which some do. Understandably, their reports back to their base in North America focus mainly on the achievements of their beneficiaries, big and small.

As I came to know more, it became clear they take no personal pride in the accomplishments; they see their role as a conduit between the folks back home and the people helped. The accomplishments are "God's work." It all seemed so different from the mainstream NGOs, religious, secular, private. Captivated, we decided to sponsor — cover the cost of school fees, uniforms and books —a couple of kids as a way to find out more. We would make a modest investment and watch from afar. That distance narrowed as we began to hear the uplifting stories of how so many lives had been changed by the Martins' ministrations.

Little did we know that we had opened the door to a flood of emails recounting how every dollar was being spent and tracing the progress of people, mostly youngsters, who didn't have a hope.

And here's the thing: in some cases, these same kids that were "without a hope" are university students or graduates now. Those emails, as well as giving supporters a ring-side seat to activities, also lent a sense of frustration. Tom's accounts are sprinkled with first names and cryptic references to interactions with these people. This creates problems when several have the same name and requires well-honed detective skills to keep pace with his bare bones accounts. In the end, though, it didn't matter whether one girl or two, or even three, were named "Barbara" or "Miriam," unless one was your sponsored child, but the Martins seemed to know who "belonged" to whom.

Nor did we foresee the ever-expanding web of supporters in Ontario and parts of the United States, places where the Martins made personal connections. More than eighty people have travelled to Peru, Uganda and Zambia so far to see for themselves the people and places the Martins describe. We went to Peru, but certainly had no intention of becoming "embedded."

So much has changed for us. At the start, I looked for cracks or inconsistencies in their story. I didn't find them. At first blush, this couple may have lacked the polish of many other missionary endeavours. They still do. But following them in person and by mail, we slowly learned that their success is anchored in their faith and the simplicity of reaching out to one person at a time.

"We love these people," Tom says often, both in presentations and conversations. That love is real, and you will see it often in the pages of this account.

A reporter told me she was drawn to the Martins because they were "so humble, sincere... honest." That was her assessment, uncoloured by religious persuasion. It made her unvarnished opinion far more valuable.

Letters addressed to "my beloved parents" scared the daylights out of me — I didn't want to get that close. Others embraced such a link, such as one couple you will meet who have sponsored, virtually adopted, youngsters from grade school to university. In fact the bond was so personal that they returned to Zambia to oversee "their girl's" entrance to university, helping to deal with both the large and mundane decisions just as they had done with their children in Canada. Or the retired businessman who opened his wallet more than once, including financing a home for orphans and covering a year's salary for the house mother.

The commitments vary, as is natural, for every supporter. However, the Martins make no discernible distinction between the committed and the lukewarm. That connection with the ever-growing HCTH mission is recounted in two or three emails a week to all, and they formed the foundation for this book. With the deluge of anecdotes came a steady flow of unanswered questions. The more information in Tom's emails, the more questions arose. My lack of knowledge was staggering, not only about their work, but about the social and economic environments in which they operated.

I needed to learn more about the countries, the economies, the governments, education systems, and social environments to understand where the Martins fit in the myriad collection of religious, charitable, and government efforts to relieve poverty and enhance education. Was there not a lot of duplication, even waste? Like sparrows feeding, we could only pick up kernels of information here and there, but not even enough to be dangerous.

This journey of discovery, however sketchy, has become an exhilarating serendipity. Wikipedia and Google have been valuable sources of information about the countries the Martins serve — Tom doesn't have time in his emails for painting the big picture — and the really remarkable work done by some fine people and organizations.

Our trip to Peru was a blended voyage, a few days to observe the Martins' work and then a week to absorb a little of the culture and history of the country. We followed the Martins to the slums, the schools, and the homes, but only as observers. Other North American visitors recount their visits as working vacations, working beside both the Martins and Peruvians (or Africans in Zambia and Uganda) in orphanages and private homes.

Peruvians are a proud, dignified and generous people. We felt like honoured guests wherever we went, and especially when we met our sponsored child, Miriam. She was then a young woman about to graduate from college, and our meeting was an unexpectedly emotional experience. After all, I had always said I didn't want to get that close.

Later that same week, a little girl called Kelly climbed up on my wife's knee. That's all it took. Now that Miriam is entering the work world, this four-year-old youngster has wiggled into Miriam's space. It won't likely be quite as hands-off as our connection was with Miriam.

The following pages cover each of the three countries in which the Martins work, highlighting differences as well as the underlying similarities — the infinite need of so many people. My observations of the work in Peru are first hand; observations on Zambia and Uganda are drawn from Tom's emails, conversations with both Tom and Cheryl, interviews with supporters who have visited one or more of the countries, and literature searches. From this review, two realities emerge: poverty is a common denominator, but each country's people embody vastly different personalities and demand individual examination.

To be sure, I also found many other stories of individuals and groups whose selfless efforts are worth recounting. Helping others is not an exclusive club — there is room for all. Finding a few of them was, in itself, uplifting, although the primary focus was on the work of Helping Cope Through Hope. Taken together, my hope is what we learned on this journey with the Martins will inspire you to see your own, unique opportunity to make a difference. Even if that means being linked with a kid so closely he or she will want to call you a "beloved parent."

Still a scary thought.

Allen Sackmann

Preface

More than 150 years ago, a little boy of ten was fired from a job of bakery delivery boy in England for being late twice. Keir Hardie was summoned to his master's dining room where he stood, soaking wet and frightfully hungry, beside a table laden with fresh breads and cakes. The monologue, according to historians, went something like this: "Boy, my customers will not stay with me if their breads are not delivered on time. To help you remember, you are dismissed, and I am withholding a week's pay."

Hardie had been detained a quarter of an hour because he was caring for a sick brother and pregnant mother, while his father prowled the streets looking for work. After being fired, Keir arrived home to a house without food, where there was now another mouth to feed. A brother had been born in his absence.

He got a job in the mines where, by the time he was thirty, he was a leader of men. He became a lay minister in the Evangelical Union, claiming: "The rich and comfortable classes have annexed Jesus and perverted his gospel. And yet he belongs to us." He became a well-known pacifist, the founder of the

Independent Labour Party in 1893, and a member of parliament during World War I.

In vast regions of the world, not much has changed in those 150 years for the poorest members of society. They are still slaves, even though their yokes of bondage may bear a different name. Lumped together, it simply adds up to destitution. Millions begin and end each day on an empty belly, finding sleep where and how they can, broken in body and spirit. Now and again, by dint of hard work, ability, or chicanery, a few can grasp and cling to a straw of hope. We hear about those.

We don't hear as much about the rest. But they are out there, Such as a Syrian boy whose legs were blown off in a civil war and who was adopted by an American woman. She said: "You can't save them all, but you can save some." The Martins share her commitment.

Chapter 1
Birth of a Mission

"WE DON'T CHOOSE. WE'LL HELP ANYONE."

— Tom Martin

In slums of Peru, or Zambia, or Uganda, you might come across a youngster named Cheryl. In fact, you might encounter more than one. You will also meet children named Tom. Like bread crumbs, the names can lead you on a trail to the places where Cheryl Martin and her husband Tom have stopped to provide food, maybe a mattress, some hygiene tips, or medical help to a pregnant teenager living on the street.

Scattering help like that is bringing to fruition a long-held goal. They worked and dreamt of the day when they could cast aside their day jobs to use their abilities to help others: the abused, forgotten, forlorn, or desperate. Christening a child with a foreign-sounding name is grateful thanks offered by the parent or parents of an infant who, along with themselves, has been embraced by people who care. They have nothing else to give to express their thankfulness.

Some of these little Cheryls and Toms live on a vast scrap heap of humanity around Peru's capital of Lima and in a place many of the city's residents don't even know exists. Manchay along with many similar slums create a necklace of desperation around the city. In Zambia, the Cheryls and Toms live near another slum on the fringe of Choma. In Uganda, they're in Namakozi, adjacent to Mityana.

When Tom talks to audiences in North America, he likes to say: "I met a little boy today named Tom… He doesn't look like me." When the titter subsides, he adds: "We are really gratified. It is no small thing to be honoured this way."

The Cheryls and Toms are joined by dozens of Hajaras in their mission story. They crop up regularly in mail and conversations. These personal glimpses reflect a passion and a yearning to help at least a few, a commitment that is almost palatable. For those who know them, it is not really a surprise, given their track record: Cheryl, a nurse, but first a stay-at-home mother of three, and caregiver for dozens of foster children and government wards, and Tom, a thirty-year veteran of classrooms and schools in east Ontario.

Like many other organizations, Helping Cope Through Hope recognizes, in the most fundamental way, that hope is the essence of well-being. For half the world, hope is relentlessly trampled by the realities of grinding poverty and oppression. No job, no money, and no food is the stew that confronts people by the generation from the oldest to the youngest in vast regions of Asia, Africa, and, to a lesser extent, South America.

In North America, we too encounter poverty with all its ugly ramifications. Crime, exploitation, and horrible neglect. Here, however, we have the means to ameliorate, if not eradicate, the impact of poverty. Many other places don't.

Some individual governments are beginning to wake up to the high cost of poverty. One of the leaders is Mexico with the *Oportunidades*, a program based on the idea that poor families can't get out of an intergenerational transmission of poverty without help. Essentially, it provides cash transfers to poor families who keep their children in school and ensure they have regular medical checkups. An accompanying requisite requires the mothers to attend workshops on subjects such as nutrition and disease prevention.

It started in 1997, with the educational element aimed at people under the age of twenty-two, beginning in the third grade of primary school through to the third grade of high school. High school support is higher for girls due to the higher likelihood of dropping out — a tendency among girls that the Martins encounter regularly.

About 30 percent of Mexico's population now is covered by the program, and the results are outstanding. Health and nutrition conditions have improved, and, most important, the number of rural children entering middle school has risen 42 percent, and high school enrolment has increased by 85 percent.

Even more dramatic, in Brazil, a program called *Bolsa Familia* (Family Grant) is credited for the drop of poverty from 22 percent of the population to 7 percent between 2003 and 2009. The income of poor Brazilians grew seven times faster than the income of the wealthy. Like Mexico, the social program is built on a cash transfer system.

A *New York Times* report by Tina Rosenberg (Jan 3, 2011) says the program fights poverty in two ways. One is straightforward: it gives money to the poor. This works. And, no, the money tends not to be stolen or diverted to the better-off. In both countries, it has reduced poverty, especially extreme poverty, "and has begun to close the inequality gap." The other way it helps is getting children into school.

Unfortunately, the improvements are not universal. In many places, corruption abounds, aided by gross incompetence, often under the gaze of the very people charged with the job of ensuring that it does not occur.

Some of those places are in Africa. National success stories are not as common there, a continent where cities and towns are growing faster than anywhere else in the world — five percent a year. That growth, without corresponding economic expansion, compounds the infrastructure challenges, beginning with the life blood of society — potable water. Its scarcity and cost exacerbate the inevitable effects of poverty. World-wide, about a billion people do not have access to consistently safe drinking water, and the situation is getting worse every day. A United

Nations study released in 2015 warns that a global water crisis is looming. In Africa, as in Asian countries such as India, it is not a crisis on the horizon, but is already a daily reality.

The World Bank is at work around the world to reduce economic inequality, provide safe water, and improve prospects for the world's poor. But the efforts are as slow as they are spotty. A generation can easily slip under bureaucratic wheels before an idea even gains traction. Intergenerational poverty thrives worldwide, even while case studies of program effectiveness pile up.

Problems abound. Bureaucratic solutions are often long on goals and short on achievement; countries wrestle with shocking bureaucratic messes, flat out corruption, wars, and natural disasters. Stripped to the basics, the plagues of poverty and disease are too big and too diverse to be solved even with bags of money.

It is a reality that weighs heavily on the conscience of many, but only a few seize the moment, despite recognizing they can't solve the worldwide problem. Just like the World Bank, but on a tiny scale, HCTH tries to improve health and living conditions while pursuing its principal goal of supporting children in school. The added dimensions go with their approach: "People we help are like our family," and "We help however we can." That might include buying chicks, getting a doctor, building a latrine, or digging a well.

Direct and immediate responses to daily needs, as they surface, is their way. Bureaucracy doesn't get a look in.

The Martins have mobilized a diverse collection of supporters, people in Canada and the United States who enable them to solve one problem at a time, but with the heaviest emphasis on education. Because of the Martins, more than 160 children are in school with a growing number in university. Because of the Martins, farming operations in Uganda and Zambia — where rural residents are among the worst off — provide homes, businesses, and wages for fifty or more families and put their kids in school. Because of the Martins, orphans have a genuine home with beds and food. Because of the Martins, family mortgages are paid off.

While their mission functions on a "right now" principle, it provides more than a glimmer of a brighter future. Some of their adoptees are graduating from school or university. Others are moving from a hand-to-mouth existence to a business. These are people who now are reaching out themselves to help others escape the pit of desperation.

Essentially, the Martins are a connection between caring North American people and suffering communities in the southern hemisphere.

Like the girl with AIDS, staring death in the face with an infant at her skirts, who first got medication, and then a job in a shop owned by a young man, who had himself earlier gotten his start with help from a Martin supporter. The ripple effect. Another graduate, with her pastor husband, has spearheaded education and spiritual training in an area that had been bereft before.

In a recent newspaper column, a naturalist wrote about the four basic habitat needs of animals: Food, water, shelter and space. Humans need that special addition of hope. HTCH adds that dimension, the spark that makes the others possible.

Is there a duplication of effort, even within the Mom-and-Pop organizations? The answer is yes, but that is also a strength. HCTH works hand-in-glove with other groups — the Martins rent their apartment in Lima from Kids Alive, participate in its programs, and provide clothing to its orphan children. It is a symbiotic relationship where, by each pursuing specific objectives, they provide greater impact. Similarly, in Africa, the Martins work side-by-side with a number of denominational groups, ranging from Catholic to Pentecostal, as well as secular groups.

Former US president Jimmy Carter, in his book *Our Endangered Values*, reminds his readers that "all major religious faiths are shaped by prophetic mandates to do justice, to love mercy, protect and care for widows and orphans, and exemplify

God's compassion for the poor and victimized." The Martins embraced that mandate from the outset.

Chapter 2
Feeling Their Way

"GOD SAID 'THIS IS WHAT I WANT.'"

— Tom Martin

The Martins' lives, from the beginning, were full of twists and turns with a missionary career a distant objective at best. The grooming for what turned out to be a second, or third, career began early and surreptitiously for this couple, who grew up not far apart in eastern Ontario.

They met as teenagers. Both were born and raised on the banks of the world-heritage Rideau Canal. Cheryl is a Hutchings, a large pioneer clan whose roots have spread wide and thick above and below Hutchings Road, a few kilometres east of Westport. Uncles, aunts, and cousins — first, seconds, and thirds — are prominent farmers and businesspeople. The one-room schoolhouse she attended has since morphed into a fishing headquarters.

Tom was minutes away in Newboro, a tiny hamlet in which he spent much of his youth. His father was a store keeper, but there was also a farm, where Tom learned about cows, pigs, and chickens, building a knowledge base that now serves him well in the agricultural areas of Africa.

Both Westport and Newboro are tourist towns. Westport is the bigger of the two, whereas Newboro has shrunk with time. Now there are only a couple of resort lodges catering to fishermen, and a meandering high-end variety store that sells everything from imported women's shoes to cedar-strip canoes. Fifty years ago, the Martin store's shelves carried mostly necessities for the farming community. A library, medical clinic, and the United Church pretty much rounded out the business sector. It is mostly the eclectic retailer that still draws shoppers and their SUVs all summer.

It was in Newboro where Tom taught Sunday School, and where he got his first taste of public speaking. He and Cheryl were married in the historic United Church just off Main Street, an event that slides into Tom's accounts of their history, a story of raising a family and pursuing careers and community service.

Tom weaves their personal histories into the presentations they make in Canada and the eastern United States. By design or by happenstance, those anecdotes draw the audiences — generally older people — into their story and the opportunity to become supporters. In church basements, community halls, or neighbourhood gatherings, they are engaged as Tom, the principal spokesperson, fills an hour with steady chatter, peppered with the names of individual recipients, as well as those of the North Americans who pay the bills.

He might start with telling that his interest in mission work was awakened by the book *Through Gates of Splendor* by Elisabeth Elliot. He gives a synopsis: Her husband and four other missionaries were murdered while working among a group of indigenous people, known to be violent, in Ecuador. He recalls that he did a review about the book in his home church. Listening, it is hard to credit the part of his memory that "I didn't like to get up and talk, [but the book] planted the desire to help people, even learn Spanish. And if I have any regrets about how life unfolded, it is that I didn't learn Spanish earlier."

He says this was his first preaching experience — "I don't know if you'd call it preaching" — although addressing an audience was a talent honed later in school classrooms. He obviously likes the stage. Cheryl says her life-long ambition was awakened early with a deep-rooted desire to help others.

Many of their public gatherings are in their hometown area, bringing together friends and relatives, so a trip into the distant past is familiar ground. In other areas, Tom has to be a bit more creative to find personal connections. But he does.

He frequently opens with a story that connects with the audience, drawing nods and smiles as memories are jogged. Then, just as they are getting comfortable, he switches gears. The audience straightens up, ears perked. The story that catches their attention might be of his seatmate on an African flight.

The woman sitting next to him was coming back to Toronto from her first visit to her homeland of Rwanda "since the troubles." As a young woman, she had been gathering firewood in the bush when she heard her family being attacked, the screams of her sister and her mother as both were raped and hacked to death, and then her father murdered. On her recent return, she says she recognized the voices of some of the attackers — "they had been our neighbours" — but she said nothing to them. "I have forgiven them," Tom quoted her as saying. "I am a born-again Christian, and I forgave them."

He clears his throat and picks up the thread of stories involving abused or neglected children, "the poorest of the poor" in three totally disparate regions in Africa and South America.

He is a short bean pole, and his scatter gun delivery fits with his tightly wound jack-in-a-box personality and energetic mind. A thought arrives and he springs into full flight, lean and fast. Sometimes, his enthusiasm gets ahead of his tongue, but it doesn't slow him a bit. A tape recorder helps to piece together how a mattress for Mary fits with a bicycle for someone, not necessarily Mary, with buying school supplies for someone, also not for Mary, and Ritah has to go to market for either clothes, or food, or both. Maybe, or maybe not, for Mary. Actually, it could be another Mary.

Cheryl fills in the gaps, corrects facts, and occasionally adds details and colour to Tom's stream of consciousness.

Slim, attractive, and slightly bowed, she easily elicits confidence. Tom credits her for managing the details of their work, such as linking by name every donor with the recipients of the money. She always has the right word, phrase or fact to help Tom out on public occasions. Speaking softly, she reins him when, like Leacock's horseman, he rides off in all directions. "Finish that story," she interjects. It is all part of an attentive support role. She greets supporters, holds aloft artwork transported to Canada for sale, and helps Tom stay within the banks of his river of words. Occasionally, she interjects a personal aside that fleshes out Tom's story, or lightens up a moment.

"I'm grateful for my white hair. People in these countries, even the young people, are very polite, so they offer a seat on the buses to old people. So I get to sit down. Tom has to stand."

In private conversations, she exhibits a quiet strength, a gracious demeanor that shows her mettle when she and Tom vie for air time. She offers, from the perspective of a mother and nurse, vivid, heart-breaking, as well as exhilarating, glimpses into the lives of people surviving on the brink. She tells of a malnourished, maltreated young woman whose husband has left her with nothing but AIDS, a youngster whose back testifies to a history of beatings, a young mother, her kids only a little younger than herself, surviving in a hovel with no food. Then she switches, telling of happy shopping expeditions for uniforms, new shoes, maybe even a present of hair ribbons as well as the feminine products that are necessary — and prized — articles for the girls.

She and Tom have so many stories and so many experiences. Tom's over-the-back-fence delivery and her timely comments magically engage the audience as eager partners. "This is an amazing story," is Tom's bridge from one story to the next, as he leads the audience through the streets and alleys. The audience follows him, in his trademark baseball cap, shorts, and running shoes, trudging along the dirty slum streets with his equally trademark smile, reaching out to one grimy urchin, patting another one on the head. In moments, the children gather and a ball appears. A game of soccer with a real ball has this sixty-six-year-old guy in a baseball cap running, shooting, and laughing with the rest of them. And, when the game is over, he may leave the ball behind. Or, as they all rest from the exertion, he'll tell them a Bible story, or teach them a song.

A long-time friend says in admiration, "It is amazing how he relates to the kids. It was a bit of an eye-opener, because Tom's teaching was high school students and he seemed to be most interested in kids ten to twelve. [But] seeing him with young children — they just come to him, they love him. He's got so much energy. He plays games with them, all the while teaching them. All kinds of kids, especially the younger ones."

On a packed bus in Lima, he spots a young boy on his mother's knee. He pulls out a sucker from his backpack, gives it to the boy and soon has both mother and child laughing as he rattles on in Spanish. Try giving a child a candy anywhere, much less on a bus, in North America!

In such personal encounters, a teddy bear or a sucker breaks down shyness. His ease with children is a genuine gift, as is the self-assurance that enables him to engage anyone, anywhere in conversation. Flying to Peru, "A family from Okotoks, Alberta, who we met on the plane, gave one hundred dollars to HCTH." Airplanes are, apparently, fertile ground for generating fresh support. On another plane trip that year, Tom's seat mates were a Canadian couple on an auditing assignment in Europe.

As invariably happens, Tom struck up an intense conversation about HCTH that ended with an exchange of email addresses. A day or two later, the Martins received word that the couple wanted to give a sizeable amount of money — $4,747 — to HCTH, enough and more than the cost of sending a student to university. The contributions — Tom calls them gifts — are still coming from the couple. What's more, a personal friendship is blossoming through home-and-home weekend visits.

His descriptions are infectious, a magnet that can easily convert a listener into a partner. Examples abound. It is easy to see how Tom, the teacher, is able to make geography and world issues come alive, as he recalls discussions and field trips on subjects as diverse as the treatment of children and women, poverty, and malnutrition.

One subject that always provokes a passionate outburst from him is the dowry system, practised extensively in Uganda, and to a lesser extent in Zambia, which might help to explain why girls so often figure prominently as recipients of Martin assistance.

"[The dowry system] is wrong. Full stop. It's wrong because, when a man pays a woman's family a cow, or a pig, or whatever, she becomes his property to do with as he pleases. She has no say. She has been bought."

His voice catches — he acknowledges that he gets emotional at times in talking about their surrogate sons and daughters — as he goes on. "We heard another sad example of cultural issues that hurt people today. A young girl HCTH helped a few years ago now is married. We learned last year that her husband beats her. Today, we asked a friend of hers why she doesn't leave him. The friend says she can't because the husband paid a dowry for her and she is his property. A dowry is common here. We have seen weddings where animals such as cows, goats, pigs, food items, etc., are given by the groom's family to the family of the bride."

It pains him that he can't do anything about this issue except rail against it; it leaves him — he with torrents of words — sputtering. Tom and Cheryl repeatedly say that they avoid making judgments of individuals, cultures or churches, but there are exceptions, such as their spirited condemnation of dowries and the prevalence of child brides.

The non-judgmental code, a guiding principle in all that they do, obviously is not something they picked up. Acceptance of others has been in the genes and it shows up throughout their lifetime.

While Tom was teaching, Cheryl made community service her personal mission. Feeding her passion for helping others, she began by providing a home to newborns waiting for adoption. A heart-wrenching job it was. The mothers, she explained, had a month in which to decide whether to keep the child or have it placed for adoption. Time enough for Cheryl to create an attachment with both, especially with women ill-equipped for motherhood. She saw them up close because the mothers could — and many did — come to the Martin home during that month as they contemplated their options.

Then, when the Martins' sons were three, six, and nine, Cheryl and Tom provided a "Children Aid's Receiving Home," to give emergency care as well as act as foster parents.

More than sixty children over the years had a safe haven under their roof. For her, their missionary careers simply turned what had been a life-long avocation into a full-time occupation. Maybe she was always unflappable, or maybe it was the steady stream of children swirling around her every day that stands her in such good stead now.

Visiting supporters of HCTH are house guests — at minimal cost — when they visit the field. Cheryl's the point person for meals and house-related chores for them, as well as the hostess when the crowds swell with locals unexpectedly stopping in. No one but the most discerning would know about the asthma or persistent back pain that slows her down as she tries to keep pace with the gazelle she married.

When closing in on retirement during the hey-day of Freedom 55, the Martins were among the age group looking down the road of healthy years and freedom from the straitjacket of regular employment. At the dinner table on the deck, they discussed their options endlessly, as long as they fit with their underlying goal.

"We always knew what we wanted to do," they agreed in recalling the discussions.

Looking back, they see now that they spent a lifetime, perhaps unwittingly, in training for "God's work." Through their early years, with three children to raise and Tom's career as a teacher to nurture, "God's work" was served through church and community activities. Cheryl's goal was deliberate when, as a mature adult, she turned to nursing and became an RN two months short of her fortieth birthday. Her eyes were set on what she called her "real calling." Meanwhile, Tom's teaching career sharpened administration skills when he moved into the principal's office with hundreds of children under his care. They were contemplating brand new careers when most of their peers were eying retirement. He was fifty-three when he cleaned out his desk. Cheryl, with one career of raising children behind her and her second in full flight, quit the hospital to embrace the third, which really was her first.

They had two compelling objectives, one crystal clear, one less so. They wanted to give back, and they wanted to help children receive an education. Life had been good. Both were in good health. The first careers of serving others were ending on a high note. The children and grandchildren lived nearby. They were blessed.

Retirement without a project would kill Tom — if it didn't kill Cheryl first. His on-off switch is stuck in the on position. It was a boon to the hundreds of kids passing through his classrooms, but it might not be a boon during retirement years.

They tested the waters as house parents in a home for unwed mothers in Macon, Georgia, which led to an invitation to stay on, primarily because of Cheryl's medical credentials and her personality — every bit the unflustered mother and nurse. Tom tutored sixty kids at an orphanage. While rewarding, these assignments left them unfulfilled. They explored possibilities with a broadcast email to about a dozen missionary organizations as diverse as World Vision and Samaritan's Purse.

"We didn't know where we wanted to go, except that it would be in Africa or South America. Who wants us?" Four responded, Africa (naturally) being the place that showed the greatest interest in them. They chose Kids Alive International, primarily because it was the first to respond, and that led them to Peru.

Their first three-month stint whetted their appetite, validated "their calling," and presented a challenge: Spanish, the language that had attracted Tom since childhood. He thrived, but Cheryl struggled. Her determination draws an oft-repeated compliment from Tom: "I was really proud of Cheryl learning Spanish."

After two years in Lima, they hooked up with a Wesleyan Church mission called World Hope International for a teaching assignment in Zambia. Through yet another connection, they were invited to Uganda to work in a children's home with many orphans. As they worked, an underlying nag kept surfacing: They were uncomfortable in large organizations.

"The idea came… it was a God thing… where this started… we don't need someone to find a place where we were needed. I guess it was God saying you don't need a big organization; you don't need someone to meet you at the airport, to prepare a place to stay. It felt like God was talking to us, 'I'm taking you to Peru, Zambia, and Uganda.'"

There wasn't, and isn't, any apparent logic to the Martins' mission field beyond what Tom and Cheryl felt was their calling.

"We said, 'Couldn't we narrow it down to one or even two countries?' and God said, 'This is what I want.'" Their work in South America and Africa, with the goal of relieving hardship while promoting the Gospel, reveals the diversities in which they find themselves. There are many.

It is telling that there is no criticism of the organizations with which they have been connected, and, in fact, they continue to maintain a loose partnership with several. Impatience with the bureaucracies and, in some cases, status symbols such as large cars used while locals walk, shaped their own approach of living much like the people they serve.

There is no question that they are missionaries, but that label is somewhat limiting, especially in light of dictionary definitions that have religious work as a dominant feature. They are missionaries with a twist, a hybrid between the secular and the religious, where looking after the earthly needs opens the door to the spiritual. Parsing the name of Helping Cope Through Hope, underscores the model of Christ whose life on earth was filled with accounts of helping anyone in need with love and compassion.

Not much overt preaching there. For the Martins, spreading the gospel is implied as they write about health, education, and providing food in the areas where they work among the most needy. In their earliest days, accounts were filled with descriptions of youngsters being drawn to them for games and songs, and then the story of Jesus. The encounters grew into bonds as the Martins helped children who needed food, or clothes, or medical treatment. They also guided likely candidates toward the school house and paid the enrolment fees. Some of those earliest "wards" are now in university, or fully self-sufficient. A few have severed their link. Most have stayed close, even though they no longer need financial help.

How do the Martins choose the people they help? That's a dilemma, since time and resources are limited. There are no official criteria. Most connections are made through word-of-mouth introductions, or through local churches. Some evolve from individuals they meet in their daily routine, such as the Muslim whose wife worked in an internet café, or the motorcycle repairman. Or, it might be a severely disabled child seen for several days in a row, holding down a corner of the curb.

"We always try to meet them in their homes [to assess their situation]," Tom explains, adding that it seems that those who attend church are more likely to want to improve their lives, "and to think like we do."

Tom says that many organizations "start at the top and work down. Not us. We started at the bottom and stay there."

With a growing number of needy children, they have had to become more selective. The issue is how to stretch the dollars to meet the continuing needs each sponsorship entails, rather than taking on even more. It is with some resignation that Tom repeats often that there are limitations to what they can do.

At a presentation, one business owner was overheard observing, "What stuck with me was that they treat everyone the same. No discrimination or judgment, just a helping hand. That lack of judgment; Christian, Muslim, whatever; it didn't matter."

He said his observation was prompted by Tom's story about a Ugandan shop keeper. There had been a casual exchange of gifts — a can of pop and a bun sent by the Martins from where they were working, with a few small bananas coming back in return.

The exchange made a connection that persisted, blossomed, and grew into a valued friendship.

It illustrates in a nutshell how they perceive their calling — needs and opportunities surround them, all waiting to be recognized, and it shows how they eased into their mission: Seeing the goals, without much thought about the route. And so it was that they kicked over the organizational traces of World Hope International and lit out on their own. Tom seems impatient with this part of the story, the tracing of their personal history and the evolution of their early missionary endeavours. He gives the impression that it detracts from the successes and accomplishments far across the sea.

From the outset, they were mandated by the HCTH Board of Directors to take others with them. By mid 2014, more than eighty supporters had spent time in the field to observe first-hand or help with whatever it was the Martins were doing. Is it possible that another spark, in another individual or couple, may be fanned into flame by the trips?

When will the Martins themselves retire from their retirement calling? Try to decode the answer. Apparently, it does not figure in their planning.

When asked one day in Manchay, as they sat in the one-room home of a family clinging to a mountain ledge, Tom said, "As long as God gives me health, I see no reason to quit." Cheryl might have had a different answer, as Tom impatiently urged her to move on. "Oh Tom, I only just sat down." God sends his messages in many ways.

Chapter 3
The Charity World

"BECAUSE HE COULD."

— Scott Harrison, founder of Charity: Water

With myriad charity organizations in Canada and the United States, the question arises as to whether there really is a need for another one or, indeed, many more. Could better results be achieved by amalgamation of similar-minded organizations?

The breadth of the industry is staggering. There are about 1.5 million charity organizations in the United States. There are 85,000 charities in Canada within the terms of the Income Tax Act, although it does not define "charity." It relies on a common law definition which outlines the purposes that cover the four "heads" of charity: the relief of poverty, the advancement of education, the advancement of religion, or other purposes that benefit the community in a way the courts have said is charitable.

In Canada, these charities employ more than two million people and account for seven percent of the Gross National Product. They come in all sizes with all sorts of goals, embracing an astounding array of interests, including one-issue pressure groups. The numbers lump together organizations as large and diverse as World Vision and the Canadian Cancer Society with a host of tiny organizations as small as a neighborhood group that cares for abandoned pets.

About a third of the Canadian charities are based in Ontario. A recent report said they declared $86 billion in revenue with all but $2 billion accounted for in expenditures. They employ 1.25 million full-time and part-time staff.

Still, one in ten Canadian children lives in poverty in one of the richest countries in the world. In the aboriginal communities, the statistic is even more shocking — one in four. The overall numbers in the United States are higher, and even these are dwarfed by the billions — yes, billions — around the world who don't have enough to eat or clean water to drink. A world-wide water crisis has already arrived in many parts of the planet. Even in North America, with its abundance of lakes and rivers, severe droughts have given residents a taste of what others are enduring — television clips of Californians turning on a tap without coaxing a drop of water from it.

When systemic poverty is fingered as the root cause of most social and health issues, how is it that societies have allowed it to continue? Even though thousands of people and billions of dollars are being spent world-wide to alleviate poverty, it seems to be a never-ending battle. Should we tackle the problem in other lands with such need in our backyard?

The simplest difference between Canada and foreign lands is that Canada has the resources to attack some of the problems. Many other countries lack a viable infrastructure and are too poor to create any kind of safety net.

These questions and related issues make it clear there is enough misery in the world to go around. Each of us is left to reach our own conclusions, but, thank God, a few individuals such as the Martins — and large organizations as well — are not satisfied to wring their hands and assuage their conscience with a donation, but rather set out to change the world for one person or one group or one community at a time.

They are driven by numbers such as these assembled by the DoSomething.org website:

- Nearly half of the world's population — more than 3 billion people — live on less than US$2.50 a day. More than 1.3 billion live in extreme poverty, less than $1.25 a day.
- 2.1 billion children worldwide are living in poverty. UNICEF estimates that 22,000 children die each day due to poverty.
- More than 1 billion people lack adequate access to clean drinking water, and an estimated 400 million of these are children. Because unclean water yields illness, roughly 443 million school days are missed every year.
- In 2011, 165 million children under the age five were stunted (reduced rate of growth and development) due to chronic malnutrition.

With these statistics rattling around in my head, I encountered Scott Harrison, the founder of Charity: Water in the book entitled *A Path Appears,* which offers a look into one of the world's most pressing issues.

Harrison is a man filled with kinetic energy.

As a young man, he was a highly successful night club promoter in New York. During an island vacation, he came face-to-face with his deep personal unhappiness and what he called "spiritual bankruptcy. I wanted desperately to revive a lost Christian faith with action." Charitable work beckoned. Most charities, however, were not drawn to a former night club promoter. He finally signed on as a volunteer on a floating hospital with a group called Mercy Ships.

In his own words on the Charity: Water website, he said: "I traded my spacious midtown loft for a 150-square-foot cabin with bunk beds, roommates, and cockroaches.

"I fell in love with Liberia — a country with no public electricity, running water, or sewage [disposal] — spending time in a leper colony and many remote villages, I put a face to [many of] the world's 1.2 billion living in poverty. Those living on less than $365 a year — money I used to blow on a bottle of Grey Goose Vodka."

He described the medical challenges encountered by Mercy doctors, and said "I met patients who taught me the meaning of courage. Many of them had been slowly suffocating to death for years and yet [were] pressing on."

It is against that backdrop, recognizing an international lack of clean water, that he formed Charity: Water. Using his impressive personal skills, he began generating support from the wealthy people he had attracted to clubs in his earlier life. That was in 2006 and, by the end of 2014, Charity: Water had spent more than $155 million on upwards of nine thousand water projects in twenty-two countries.

He says, "For me, charity is practical. It is sometimes easy, more times inconvenient, but always necessary. It is the ability to use one's position of influence, relative wealth and power to affect lives for the better. Charity is singular and achievable."

In *Our Endangered Values*, President Carter entitled one chapter "The World's Greatest Challenge in the New Millennium" and identified that challenge as poverty in whatever form it appears. The Carter Center, founded by President and Mrs. Carter in 1982, has launched wide-ranging health and social programs in more than eighty countries, including more than thirty-five in sub-Saharan Africa.

The Carter Center's objective is to advance peace and health world-wide. One of its signature achievements has been "leading a coalition that has reduced incidence of Guinea worm disease from an estimated 3.5 million cases in 1986 to 126 today."

The Carter Center's reach is huge, from monitoring elections, to fighting disease, to equipping people to help themselves and against a backdrop in which "the possibility of failure is an acceptable risk."

Another statement that resonates particularly in the context of HCTH is: "Our Center's programs have shown that with wise use of even limited resources, extremely poor people demonstrate remarkable intelligence, innovation, and effectiveness." The Center has 150 staff, "local citizens, whom we train, must perform the necessary tasks and be paid by their own government. We found them to be very dedicated and competent."

So, at opposite ends of the spectrum, in terms of money invested and reach, are the Martins, Jimmy Carter and Scott Harrison. But they have much in common. Both HCTH and Water: Charity spend every dollar publicly raised for helping individuals and communities. Neither use donations to pay for administration. Harrison has private donors to pick up operating costs; the Martins pay them themselves. All three organizations are anxious to equip the poor to help themselves.

Harrison reaches into the Bible, just as the Martins and Carters do, to buttress his approach to charity with the example of the Good Samaritan who told the innkeeper to spend whatever was necessary until the victim was better.

"Because he could."

He quotes Colossians 3, which enjoins readers "to put on charity, which is the bond of perfection." Harrison says, "Although I'm still not sure what it means, I love the idea. To wear charity."

So, however you wear it, where ever you wear it, charity becomes you. Giving is enjoyable and living your charity is rewarding.

Chapter 4
In the Beginning

"IT BEGINS WITH SOMEONE CRYING
AND SOMEONE ELSE HEARING."
— Rob Bell, *Jesus Came to Save Christians*

Sometimes, there's a feeling or notion that keeps crowding into one's mind. It starts with an idea, a reoccurring thought. And sometimes you can't shake it. The Martins had lots of time on long aeroplane rides and in airport departure lounges — travel from Zambia or Uganda back to Canada is often a thirty-hour door-to-door adventure — to think about the charitable organizations they were working for and others they observed. The questions persisted, at first just between Tom and Cheryl, and then spreading to trusted friends. Couldn't more money go to helping people if the overhead was reduced? Should land bought with charity dollars be left idle while people are hungry? Should foreigners drive shiny cars when locals walk?

Was there a better way?

A quick glance at 2014 financial statements of two charities gives a hint of the Martins' discomfort. World Vision, which is active in about one hundred countries, collected $1,038 million for supporting its objective of "working with all of the most vulnerable regardless of religion, race, ethnicity or gender." It spent about 15 percent — $167 million — on fund-raising and general administration.

On a smaller scale, and closer to home for the Martins, was World Hope International (WHI), the organization sponsored by the Wesleyan Church, their own denomination. World Hope works in "fourteen of the poorest countries," and is guided by a Bible verse (Matthew 25:40, NIV) which says "whatever you did for one of the least of these brothers of mine, you did for me." Lined up against World Vision, WHI is small potatoes with its $4.7 million in total revenue, of which 19 percent was allocated to administration (11 percent) and fund-raising (8 percent) in 2014. Its mission statement commits the organization to work in vulnerable and exploited communities to alleviate poverty, suffering, and injustice. It adopts a holistic approach aimed at providing clean water, employment opportunities, education, and freedom from slavery.

The Martins' discomfort couldn't be cast aside, even though they had no axe to grind with the large organizations. After all, with half the world population living on less than $2.50 a day and millions dying of starvation or malnutrition, there is certainly work to do. But for them, it wasn't quite right. Tom would describe it as "a God thing," the phrase he uses with conviction, as he gives credit to God for connecting the dots.

Sometimes, those dots are far apart, separated by miles and even years, but, with the benefit of hindsight, they can make out how their charity came together.

In March, 2005, they returned to Canada convinced that God wanted them to work in the three countries they had visited. They also felt they could be more effective without the constraints and hierarchy of recognized charities. By the time the plane landed, the ideas began to take shape.

They hit the tarmac brimming with ideas. They'd form their own organization and get their friends to help. As the notion jelled, two unconnected series of events loomed large.

The first had its roots years ago in Tom's geography classroom. He proudly recounts how the geography section in his school was renowned for its excellence. Part of it, he now says, came from the frequent field trips teachers organized for their students. He himself led students on trips in Ontario, New York State, and even once to Italy. "It was a new experience for them, and I enjoyed seeing them enjoying the things they were seeing and doing. For many, they had never been out of their own province, let alone country. Their horizons, as well as their knowledge, were broadened."

Why wouldn't the same benefits accrue to supporters of charities who could make "field trips" to experience first-hand the challenges, results, and rewards achieved through their active involvement in a foreign environment?

The second defining set of circumstances evolved from a situation while they were working for an established mission organization. A woman well-known to the Martins asked them if her son — a former student of Tom's who had been cared for by Cheryl as an infant — could visit and work with them for a short time. She thought it would be a valuable experience. The mission administrators said no, apparently on religious grounds. The boy was not from the "right" denomination and may not have even attended church.

"He was a good kid. I coached him in soccer. Cheryl knew him well, and that rejection stuck with us. So, when we set up Helping Cope Through Hope ... we decided to invite people to come with us — we really enjoy people — and, second, that we would not discriminate against anyone."

They also agreed that there would be a proviso attached: their fellow travelers would, just like the Martins, pay their own expenses. "I mean, we'd have to eat at home, so why wouldn't we pay our own costs when we were away?"

Armed with the three principles — accompany the Martins, no discrimination, pay your own way — they floated their ideas around their church, their circle of friends, and their business associates. The response to their mission concept was good enough to keep them forging ahead, gathering information and advice, although several wondered why the Martins would want to work in three countries. "Pick one" was a frequent suggestion.

They were also warned that winning government approval of a new charity could take up to two years, a caution flag attached to any project with potential government involvement. Hate it if you want, they were cautioned, but the wheels of bureaucracy grind exceedingly slow, including the wheels of Revenue Canada, the government department which assesses charitable status. The assigned number, which allows donations to be eligible for taxation deductions, is a coveted and zealously protected thing.

Criticizing government, particularly the taxation wing, is a Canadian pastime, but the Martins' experience undercut the stereotype: "The people there were very helpful. They helped a lot."

To begin, the Martins needed a name, a constitution and a board of directors. Mulling over words and phrases that might work for a name, two words kept cropping up, including one that was a stranger in Tom's lexicon — cope. People could cope with life if they had hope. Tom's vision was to reach people who frequently viewed life as hopeless. He recalled reading *The Purpose Driven Life* by American preacher Rick Warren, which included the statement, "You need hope to cope," which led to Helping Cope Through Hope. The Martins tested the phrase on their local pastor, who was encouraging. Then they unveiled it to the group that would become the organization's founding directors.

Focussing on hope as a core value was a stroke of genius — "a God thing." The book, *A Path Appears,* devotes a compelling chapter to the subject of hope, saying that humans anywhere in the world can be locked in a poverty trap of despair and depression. It builds on specific examples of the transformations that can occur when hope is injected into the lives of poor and neglected people.

With the name chosen, Helping Cope Through Hope needed a constitution. Tom put pen to paper. Eighteen pages later, including one revision requested by Revenue Canada, the document was done.

Tom recalls, proudly: "We got a letter saying we could begin giving receipts for charitable donations Sept. 1, 2005." Less than four months from start to finish, a bureaucratic miracle. In more recent times, such speed is unlikely. Since 2012, bureaucrats have been scrutinizing charities to ensure they meet established criteria. Many groups have lost their status, a situation that has continued to provoke simmering discontent and complaints well into 2014.

When they were collecting ideas and suggestions for their organization, a recurring question was why they were planning to work in three countries.

"We continued to have second thoughts when people asked if we couldn't narrow the number of countries." In the end, they relied on their sense of divine leading, buttressed by the alacrity with which the government handled their charity application.

On June 11, 2005, a Saturday morning, sixteen individuals including the Martins gathered in the Roblin Wesleyan Church hall, where they spent several hours in a fine-tooth review of Tom's eighteen pages. By the time they left, a non-profit, non-partisan, voluntary Christian outreach organization was born, and they were founders. The directorate shrank to a more manageable ten, later.

As they readied to leave, Tom repeated the goal of Helping Cope Through Hope, to foster hope by helping people cope with daily life, through the provision of food, medicine, housing, education, or any other need identified by the Martins. No constraints, no criteria, no oversight. The new board agreed, testimony to the trust the Martins had earned with their history of action.

The articles of incorporation are unadorned and wonderfully simple. No lawyer plugged legal loopholes or potholes. Malfeasance never entered the founders' heads, although a director or staff member can be removed if he/she persists "in any form of misconduct that tarnishes the work or reputation of Helping Cope Through Hope and causes disrepute to the name of our Lord Jesus Christ...." Removal from office would be the final step in a process where the individual is "disciplined according to the Biblical principle: disciplining in love." The subject is accorded only eight lines, whereas the statement of faith, which clearly defines belief and doctoral positions, covers a page and a half.

The last clause could also be the statement of work:

"We believe that the Christian life is lived by trust in Christ and under the fellowship with Him, for He is 'the way, the truth and the life.' The Christian life, we believe, manifests itself in service to God and service to fellow men of all races and stations of life. This is summed up in the two great commandments. We must love God with all our hearts, souls, minds and strength. We must also love our neighbours as ourselves."

To support that work, the mandate is "to relieve social and economic conditions experienced by the poor ... to advance Christian faith through Bible studies and evangelism ... to provide basic health care, education and medical supplies ... [and] to undertake all such other things as are ancillary or incidental to the attainment of the objectives."

The constitution is also unambiguous on the spiritual status of directors: "born-again Christians." But Tom says, "We don't and can't judge how anyone lives." It is an attitude that is soaked into the fabric of the organization so that it is implicit — not explicit — in the stories they tell. A born-again Christian is one who accepts Christ as a personal saviour and commits to follow his example in daily living.

Tom and Cheryl like describing how they navigated those uncharted waters in the early days, and still glow in the excitement of it ten years later.

"Revenue Canada asked how much money we expected to raise in the first year," recalls one before the other takes over. "We didn't have any idea of what would be reasonable." Back to the first: "Maybe $10,000." The other: "You know how much was given? Sixty thousand dollars that first year."

Then, just two and a half weeks after the inaugural meeting, their local church hosted a dinner and silent auction. Neighbour Debbie Neff, the organizer, was overwhelmed by the response. She had set her sights on about one hundred donations. Reality produced about double that. Plans called for one hundred dinner guests, and one hundred forty tickets were sold in advance. "It surpassed anything I could have imagined," she said. The Martins and HCTH directors were encouraged to explore other possibilities in a typically small-town approach to fund-raising. A meeting agenda that fall mentioned pizza kits, a cookbook, dinners, penny jars, and "other ideas." Among the results of activities pursued, a gospel sing raised $1,000, and the cookbook was popular enough to warrant a second printing.

Most of the support base came from community churches — four of the founding directors were clergymen drawn from the area around Greater Napanee, a bustling town of 15,000, located on the eastern tip of the Bay of Quinte, twenty-five miles west of Kingston, Ontario. First settled by Empire Loyalists in 1784, today it is home to at least sixteen churches.

Publicity, or promotion, was barely considered during the formation stages, and still isn't — officially. Yet, local media was unstinting in its coverage of the start-up, with features, photographs, and announcements. "Tired of High Overhead, couple starts own aid agency" —*Kingston Whig-Standard*, May 17, 2005; "Tamworth couple creates hope through helping" —*Napanee Beaver*, May 4, 2005; "Tamworth couple founded voluntary outreach organization" —*Journey*, a publication of the Roman Catholic archdiocese of Kingston, October-November, 2006.

Reporter Meghan Balogh of the *Napanee Guide* says she tends to report at least annually on the Martins' activities, attracted because they are "unassuming, very honest. They give an impression that they are embarrassed to be talking about themselves rather than their work." Ms. Balogh adds she does not hold the same religious persuasion as the bulk of Martin supporters.

Radio and television, too, saw value in the Martins' work. Volunteers with promotion savvy jumped in to create a website and produce increasingly sophisticated brochures and presentation tools. A university professor far removed from the Napanee area produced a professional slide show.

"I think I would pay for [the promotional tools] myself before I would change that," says Tom, as he reflects on how promotional materials are made without cost to HCTH, helping to maintain the determination that none of the donations coming in would be siphoned off for overhead expenses. No big organization, no big fund-raising campaigns, no administrative team. Nothing beyond Tom, Cheryl, a volunteer treasurer ("she's a god-send"), and a board of directors that meets twice a year.

In their 2013 annual report to the board, Tom reported total HCTH administration charges of $250.12. All the rest of the $130,000 raised went directly to recipients in the field. Eighteen areas of work were recorded, ranging from helping children go to school, starting individuals in business, taking supplies and materials to the field, building homes and schools, visiting the sick and, "helping the elderly, who are often neglected."

Since 2008, HCTH has joined the charities that offer gift certificates. As well as working "gifts," the certificates are popular with individuals who want to direct precisely where their money goes. The options are: mosquito net, $10; blanket, $10; mattress, $30; backpack for school supplies, $20; clothing for one person, $20; Bible, $10; food (beans, corn, rice, bananas, or sugar), $20; medical supplies, $20; sponsorship of a child, $360 a year.

Often, the Martins return to Canada with photos for donors that feature a piglet under someone's arm — a pig bought with a gift certificate. Another might be a grinning Peruvian boy cuddling a baby rabbit. In 2013, the Martins had the job of carrying out specific instructions attached to the $5,700 in gift certificates.

One email reported that they had sufficient certificate money to buy — and give away — forty pigs and goats. Another from Zambia, reported that the Martins were able to buy three bicycles, three mattresses, two beds, eight Bibles, chickens, food, and medical supplies.

While the Martins are scrupulous in accounting how donated money is spent, they make no mention of their own expenses, implicitly assuming that it is unnecessary. Their own expenses run between $12,000 and $15,000 a year, and are covered by their pensions and savings. (Our rent for a week with the Martins in Lima was thirty dollars a night.) In those first heady days of the organization, the Martins seemed to mimic the approach of others in the field. Slowly, their own personalities began to emerge, both in what they did and how they did it. Early emails talked most often about providing food, medicine, clothes, and introducing several youngsters to school. By way of explanation they still say, "We are attracted to the underdog," and, "We want to be part of the neighbourhood." In Africa, they deliberately live among the people they serve, and are undaunted as they visit families in their homes.

"It doesn't matter if there are holes in the couch, or not enough chairs, or whatever. We're just blessed by being there with them. And we think they are too."

In contrast, Tom talks about aid representatives driving new cars. Africans in need don't drive cars, so the Martins walk, ride bicycles, or ride an ancient motorcycle, just the way the locals do. And he illustrates the impact of their approach with a story from those first days on their own in Zambia. When the father in one of the families they had befriended died, the Martins grieved with the family, the only white people in the procession walking the mile to the cemetery. Nothing speaks louder than actions, and suddenly, or perhaps not so suddenly, the Martins found that they had been accepted.

"They saw that we really loved them. They weren't leery anymore."

Chapter 5
Pearson Airport

"VIEW BAGGAGE ALLOWANCES."

— Air Canada Instructions

Toronto's International Airport is the second most active airport in North America for international travel, sixty-five airlines carrying 35 million people in 2012. Its Terminal 1 is a constantly noisy polyglot, reflecting the varied origins and destinations of its travellers. Pearson is its name, honouring arguably one of Canada's most influential citizens of the twentieth century. Professor, civil servant, statesman, and diplomat before becoming Prime Minister, Lester Pearson received the Nobel Peace Prize for his work in resolving the Suez Canal crisis in 1957.

Mr. Pearson had an unassuming nature and an abiding desire to improve the lives of others, as demonstrated by his social record as prime minister. And so it seems fitting that it is through these portals that the Martins set out twice a year — October and January — to make a difference in somebody's life. Getting a mattress to sleep on is no less a gift for an individual than universal health care for a nation.

Overseas flights from Toronto, particularly to Africa and
Asia, turn Terminal 1 into a zoo of kids, luggage, and languages.
Airline staff, many wearing pasted on smiles, drift through
to help.

It is all old hat to Tom and Cheryl as they herd their bags on
carts, plus carry-ons at their feet, toward the check-in counter.
It might be old hat, but it is still an anxious process, one largely
of their own making. Over the years, their notes and emails
describe variations of the scene played out many times. But
there are recurring themes that can provide a composite view
that may go something like this:

"Where are you going?" asks the agent as Cheryl slides
passports across the counter. "Lima, eh? Put the bags on the belt
one at a time." She peers over the edge of the counter, raises an
eyebrow and checks the scale. The fourth time, she lifts a hand.
"It is way overweight. What's in it?"

"Clothes, teddy bears," says Tom. "To give away. We're
missionaries." He rarely misses a bet to promote their cause.
"We go every year to work in poor communities, helping kids
with clothes and books to go to school. Not just kids, but we
help mothers who need food…."

In a world of too many passengers and too many passports,
the explanation can break through the monotony of the agent's
job and achieve a hint of interest. Or not. The Martins still often
hear: "Well, that bag is too heavy; you'll have to take some
stuff out."

"What can I do with it?" Tom counters "Some poor soul
needs those clothes. I can't just leave it."

"Well, you'll have to pay overweight charges."

"Okay, but that means there is less money to buy food for
a destitute family where maybe someone has AIDS, or a father
who has disappeared."

He's still talking as the agent tags the last of the bags and,
more often than not, offers a tired, "We'll let it go."

In Tom's own words, from 2014:

Dear friends and family: It is 6:45 a.m. at an airport hotel in Toronto. I will go on the shuttle bus at 8 to the airport ... I am flying on Ethiopia Air for the first time. It is a fourteen hour and twenty-minute flight to Addis Ababa, Ethiopia, then a two hour wait, then a two hour and twenty minute flight to Entebbe. My friend Joram is meeting me there. I was thinking it would be a normal arrival day after getting money changed in Kampala and buying a few groceries then arriving in Mityana about five p.m.

Pray for this day. I have always said that the most stressful time of the whole trip is the airport experience upon departure. This is because we always have at least one extra suitcase. The suitcases are at maximum weight or a little over. My carry-on is much overweight. My personal bag has a laptop, a Bible and much else so it is heavy also. It is a bit uncomfortable with four layers of shirts and long pants over shorts but my feeling is that my little bit of uncomfortableness is nothing compared to the people the extra pants and shirts will go to. Actually, Cheryl is probably thinking that something is wrong with me, because I usually have two long pants over shorts and five layers of shirts, which includes a sweatshirt and coat. This time I shed the sweatshirt. I did bow to the season and warm temperatures. One heavy coat does look a bit out of place but people don't know where I am going.

Thank you for praying on Tuesday as I went to the airport. Things went smoothly. They did weigh my carry-on. After taking out my Bible to carry, [the carry-on] was [still] overweight but ok. Then they weighed my backpack. Overweight again but I took out a couple of heavy items to carry and still over but ok. Around the corner the items went back where they originally were.

(On one occasion, a ticket agent, as she tagged the last bag, smiled slightly and asked, "How many shirts, exactly, are you wearing?")

Thank you for your prayers. I arrived safely in Uganda tonight after a bit of an adventure. The plane from Ethiopia to Uganda left on time at eleven a.m., travelled about fifteen feet and stopped never to roll again. After an hour of trying to fix it we were taken

off, given a meal and waited five and a half hours for another
plane. The plane was supposed to land in Uganda at one p.m. but
landed at six thirty.

Preparations for every trip are arduous, and the Martins
know baggage allowances off by heart. Surrounded by mounds
of shirts, pants, and toys, the challenge is to winnow them down
while visualizing the potential recipients. One bag, for one trip,
included six infant sleeper sets, a dozen tee-shirts, a package of
baby wipes, a collection of girls' shorts and tops, six tennis balls,
a dozen baseball caps with logos ranging from sports teams to
beer brands, three pairs of new clogs (pink, green and blue), two
pairs of women's shoes, and a brand new duffle bag. Teddy bears
are squeezed, scrunched, and twisted into the tiniest of space,
because Cheryl knows a lot of little people who will literally love
them to bits as the first thing many of these children have ever
owned that would be hers/his alone.

On an early trip to Peru, the Martins took a picture of teddy
bears displayed on furniture around their living space — more
than three hundred. Many would reappear much later, worse
for wear, hugged close by their owners. Other pictures show a
smiling, bright-eyed baby waving from a soft and cozy bunting
bag or an older person proudly smiling in a blouse or shirt —
maybe Caribbean colours.

The distribution of the clothing and toys is a carefully
measured process. As the Martins settle into their
accommodation in each country, bags are unpacked and items
stacked, much like a commercial shop. Then, as they begin to
make their rounds, the first order of business is to determine
whether individuals to be visited are in need of "gifts." The
merchandise is parsed out slowly, until near the end of their
stint in each country, an email may announce that they only
have a couple of tee shirts or caps left.

And it gives them pleasure to report back that they
encountered someone wearing a hockey jersey or a little league
baseball cap. A leather jacket with the name of a Napanee player
stopped Tom in his tracks. The player — not the guy wearing

the jacket — had been one of his students. The beer shirts seem somewhat out of place, although they may testify to the non-discriminatory approach to their work.

Seeing the appreciation of an individual receiving a jacket or skirt, the joy of a child receiving his or her first new toy, makes the airport tensions all worthwhile. The luggage anxiety accompanies every trip to the airport, and the Martins still scheme to get the bags through intact.

On one journey, Tom said he went to the airport with some "self-made stress," and no wonder: "It was warm with, two pairs of shorts, four shirts, a hoodie, and carrying a heavy leather coat. To help, in case the suitcases were weighed, I had the coat sleeves full of heavier items, such as my camera, a bag of trail mix, etc."

His computer bag "was heavy with three books, two Dell computers, and other items."

Then, there was the joy at the other end, when they took inventory of their bloated bags. "But we didn't have to pay extra. Praise the Lord."

Chapter 6
Part of the Family

"YOUR WORTH IS NOT BASED ON WHAT
YOU HAVE OR WHO YOU ARE BUT ON WHAT
OTHERS BECOME BECAUSE OF YOU."

— A HCTH graduate

It doesn't take much to become part of the Martin network. An expression of interest and you are in, a recipient of regular accounts of achievements, failures, routines, and minutia in the world of HCTH. It has been ever thus, a trademark of the Martins' approach, where every supporter is a day-to-day partner in their work.

Setting up housekeeping in 2006 in Uganda revealed that the fridge didn't work in their new quarters, "but we got another that keeps things slightly cool. Praise God that two of the burners on the stove work and the oven works — if we can find the racks." They had no washing machine, but did have a clothesline.

"Things are great here," Tom said with customary enthusiasm. "We live in a neat area near town, but still in the country." There were times, though, when a hint of frustration crept in, especially in dealing with African bureaucracy.

Every couple of days on average, although sometimes more frequently, Tom writes to "friends and family" with streams of consciousness reporting, dashed off at speed after a long, activity-packed day. No one knows when electricity and/or the internet may fail.

"Power is on, PTL. Power went off at nine p.m. last night and was off until two thirty p.m. today," said one message, which helps explain why, in his haste, some snippets of encounters with people and places only connect in his mind.

And another day: "I have to be quick. The Internet is down and I have to use the phone line [to send emails]."

And another: "The power just went off."

These messages provide an unvarnished portrait of the Martins' day-to-day life, their tasks, their victories, and their disappointments. In the reading, there is anticipation in knowing that, likely, a story later will fill in the blanks around a name plunked in without the context. Just be patient, and the picture will appear.

Good humour and plentiful patience show up regularly in the emails. "Our water was off for twenty-four hours. There was a problem with the pump. We got along okay. Fortunately, I had just had a bath."

Take it as it comes. More than one account explains that weak electrical service meant Cheryl held a candle while Tom typed — until the computer battery was drained. In Uganda, he tries to write his emails early, before the sun sets, because of the unpredictable electrical service. Sometimes, it can be too weak to power a light bulb. And another complaint: taking stock of the day's activities was difficult, even when the lights are on, because, "It is hard to remember everything we did today."

Those emails transport the reader to wherever the Martins are, showing the faces they see, the dusty — or muddy — roads, the compassion or disappointments. Grace Bresee, a cousin of Cheryl's, is one of a handful who has saved many of them, beginning in 2005. She had more than 600 by mid-2014.

Linking the references is a "Where's Waldo?" process, but assuredly, by diligent searching, eureka moments arrive. And those, in their own right, renew excitement in the story itself. Maybe that's part of the communication strategy. Catherine was one of the girls in the HCTH network. She had cropped up in messages, often without context. Tom rolled some of the references to Catherine together in a 2014 bundle, fleshing out their private exchanges, which would be similar to those of most parents with an absentee daughter. They illustrate, in practical terms, how the Martins interact with and support the many children that have become part of the family.

Catherine is an orphan. Her mother died two weeks after she was born, and her father died when she was ten, leaving her to live on the streets, or with whoever would take her in, where, as is somewhat typical in her Zambian culture, she was abused, physically, and sexually. Her horrible life drove her out of school in Grade Four, even though primary education is a government requirement. Unfortunately, that requirement is ignored if school fees and related costs are not paid. Government enforcement is lackadaisical at best.

"When we met her, she was put in Grade Seven, because that was the only opening. She has struggled in school, but when we are there, we read with her each night," using a *Good News* Bible and other books. Reading, however, was difficult, painful, and slow — "She barely knew the words. She was reading at maybe a Grade One level."

Tom explained that their email exchanges from when the Martins return to Canada serve both as a way of staying close and a way to help her improve her English. The goal was to ready her for the national examination at the end of Grade Nine, which is in English, and is required to continue into secondary school.

March 29, 2013, was a day like Catherine had never had before. Tom and Cheryl had a young Canadian girl named Kirsten with them for a few weeks as she completed some high school course work. Kirsten conspired with the Martins to give Catherine her first-ever birthday party. (Catherine's actual birth date is approximate.) There was a cake, candles, ice cream, and balloons. Maybe a few guests. Such a party. And then the roof fell in.

Shortly after the birthday party, Catherine went to the hospital, complaining of feeling ill and experiencing unexplicable bleeding. The Martins hurried to the hospital to see her, but she turned her back and wept. Through her sobs, she said they wouldn't love her any more. Unmarried, pregnant, she had had a miscarriage.

"It was a chance to show unconditional love," said Tom. "I said 'Catherine, we still love you. It doesn't matter what's happened. We love you.'"

Emails kept them close when the Martins returned to Canada, as well as improving Catherine's English. Tom transcribed her messages to help readers understand her spelling — fortes is fortress, leaned is learned; fast is first and inverted is invited — but most were easily overlooked. Beneath the surface is recognition of a greater need — this neglected orphan needs, as much as anything, regular reassurance of familial affection. Having once tasted it, she wasn't about to let it go.

Her story unfolds in the emails and includes many references to Klaus, whom she calls papa. He had come to Zambia from Germany to work with an NGO, and Catherine, before she met the Martins, used to loiter near where he lived. One January morning, Catherine knocked on his door and asked if he would help her. Klaus arranged with a pastor, and the Martins, to put her in school, and a friendship evolved with the Martins also. Klaus was introduced in Martin emails as a farmer with a 3,600 hectare (8,000 acres) farm, which the Martins visit periodically. One visit was obviously a treat, because Tom described a barbecue dinner comprising fish, chicken, and German sausage, adding "this was our first meat feast in 2014."

Tom's assessment of Klaus' role with Catherine is that it has been "a great blessing" to her and the bond is evident in the following exchange between Catherine and the Martins

Hello Tom and Cheryl

how are you today, and how is Canada? We are fine, me and papa. We miss you a lot. I have loved this story video so much it is so nice. [The video features the exploits and impressive accomplishments of a legless gymnast] *and I can even cry she so beautiful and you can see how God blessed her, ya [yes] it can happen in the name of our Lord Jesus. I am on the farm today, cause we have holiday. many greetings from papa to everybody there. I will write you again the email this afternoon.:good morning*

Catherine

Dear Catherine:

It is so good to hear from you too. It rained a lot yesterday but is nice right now. It is seven a.m. on Sunday morning ... we are going to Cheryl's brothers. There is a family dinner. All of Cheryl's family will be there... There will be about sixty people.

Our summer has been cooler and rainier than normal. I like it warmer. It is always great to hear from you. We love you and pray for you often. That girl in the video is amazing.

Love, Tom and Cheryl

Dear Tom and Cheryl

How are you today, and how is your family doing? we are doing good. It is so good to hear from you always. that girl is so amazing so blessed from God. Here in Zambia it's starting getting hot and hot. And Klaus was asking if you can ask Kirsten's Father reply his

*email please cause it is so important for him please Tom can you
do that for papa? please many greetings from papa and I.*

love Catherine, Sometime but a lot

Dear Catherine:

*I did email Kristen's father. His name is Karl. Hopefully he
emails Klaus.*
*Are you in school now? Today after we go for a walk we will
pick beans, broccoli and dig potatoes from our garden.*
Have a great day!

Love, Cheryl and Tom

The Martins took such great pleasure and encouragement
from the next email that they decided to include it as the last
one in the collection they aggregated.

Dear Tom and Cheryl

*good morning, how are you today? And how was your game went
did they won your friends? How is Cheryl doing tell her that I
miss her so much I wish she would be here now in Zambia. Say
hello to your family and everybody there.*
*Last week we had church meeting at Fortes mission world
hope. I don't know how to write this, but you know what I mean.
It was good for Cause I never been in that meeting before, we
leaned (learned) about God, how to forgive someone, how to be
purer in our heart and also not to keep the anger inside our heart
because if we keep the anger in our heart, then God cannot forgive
us so I leaned (learned). I have also meet a lot of new friends from
USA all thou (although) I was skilled (scared) to go there cause
it was my fast (first) time to go there. I was inverted (invited) by
my new Friends you know them already Courtney and Jeremy
[World Hope missionaries] you meet them here in the mission.*

And Courtney also helped me on my exams test she is helping me in English, maths and others. she good to me and her children also there good to me. So I had a good time on the church meeting, very fun. have good day

love Catherine

Catherine, of course, is not the only "family member" who sends the Martins emails. She competes for air time with Joram, Barbara, Annet (several), Kenneth, Fenister and who-knows-how-many others from among the hundreds of individuals who are helped by HCTH.

For example: "We received good news from Beatrice, who got her results from Grade Nine. She did very well…. Beatrice is a girl who never went to school until we met her at age eleven. She skipped Grades One, Three, and Five to catch up to her age. She has been number one in her class except for last year when she was number Two in a bigger school."

These individual exchanges, plus the steady stream of emails to supporters, turn Tom's letter-writing into a herculean task that he tackles at night after a packed day. It is little wonder he doesn't have time to give the back stories of all the people in his reports, such as explaining how "Little Earl" got his name when reporting that the boy had fallen, "and his arm was very swollen and twisted. He had broken it, but his mother had not taken him to the hospital until today. It had to be very painful." It takes a ream of emails, spread over weeks, to get the rest of Earl's story.

Earl is not a common name in Zambia. It was the name of a long-time friend of Tom's who had travelled to Zambia three times to work with the Martins. Little Earl's mother, Naomi, lived with her little boys near another family being helped by HCTH and was drawn into the Martins' net. She was always happy and grateful for the assistance her sons received from Tom's friend Earl, who had a great affection for them, as well as a deep-seated fondness for Zambia. He died in 2010, and his three sisters decided to honour his memory by sponsoring a child. And that's how Little Earl got his name, but his mother calls him "Triple Earl." The Martins are not sure why but, possibly, it is in recognition of the three sisters of the Canadian Earl.

And interspersed in those messages are the random thoughts that illustrate the complex decisions related to their work. Alongside Earl, a recalcitrant water pump, multiple school fees, and construction to oversee, Tom drops into the email:

"A man came to our door yesterday. He wants to talk to us. His wife died two months ago, leaving a young baby. Pray for wisdom in our decisions."

Another heart-wrenching case. "We need wisdom in dealing with a family in a bad state. We have helped them a lot and they are good people. The father died two years ago of AIDS. The wife and three children were then tested. The wife and middle child are HIV positive. The mother is not well, and in November she was in hospital for three weeks. They did not know if she would live. The issue is how best to help them when we are not here, especially if three young children have no mother or father. God will work this out."

Chapter 7
The Ugandan House Girl

"BUT I WORK HARD."

— Hajara

The well that served Hajara's household was a kilometre away from the house. Every morning, it was her job to walk down the hill with two empty twenty-litre water jugs and then lug them, full, back up the hill to the house. Often, she would be beaten for her efforts. Hajara was ten years old, maybe. She wasn't sure. Whatever her age, she was a little kid.

Tom made the trek with her one day to learn why she was so often abused. She explained that men who sold water came with large containers and chased away the little kids like her while they filled their barrels. But if Jane, the lady of the house, felt Hajara had taken too long, the lazy, slothful child would be beaten for her tardiness. In recounting the story, Tom allows that even a fit and wiry adult (him) found the two jugs so heavy that he had to take breaks in hauling them up the hill. "She was very strong." He added that he and Cheryl had their own experience of fetching drinking, cooking, washing, and bathing water by the bucket from wells which felt farther away on the return trip than they were on the outgoing one. And discovering to their dismay how much water is really needed every day.

"Hajara, why are you beaten?" he asked as they walked.

"Because I take too long. She says I don't do good work, but I work hard." The voice was flat, emotionless, as she recounted her life from when she was about seven — an approximation — when she became a house girl for Jane and her husband, who happened to be Hajara's brother. Her story is commonplace; house-girl-ship is endemic among the poor in both Uganda and Zambia, where the importance of having one less mouth to feed makes loaning out little girls a common choice.

The Martins knew Jane's household, having previously sponsored two of her children into the school system, when they became aware of this other youngster. It appeared that Hajara didn't go to school; she hung back with watchful, sad eyes. On their visits to the family, the Martins ensured that Hajara also got small gifts of dolls and clothes, just like the other girls. In the process, they gained permission from Jane to have Hajara join the others in the school system.

The Martins bought the books, uniforms, shoes, and socks, paid the fees, and left Uganda with the satisfaction of having opened a door of education for another youngster. But when they returned a year later, a friend reported that Hajara hadn't shown up at school very often and had eventually dropped out completely. Turned out, Hajara would get locked in the house so that neighbours would think she was in school. She'd also been warned not to talk to the Martins.

In these neighbourhoods, there are eyes everywhere, but walls of silence; minding your own business, especially around foreigners, is endemic. But the Martins' hummingbird approach — putting a child in school here, buying medicine there, sending maize somewhere else — often wins them an entry into local confidence based on performance. Still, wariness, even suspicion exists. They are on trial every day.

The Martins visited the school's head master, whom they had previously helped by paying for some school materials. He verified details of Hajara's absences and agreed to arrange for her to meet the Martins at a spot away from prying eyes. The youngster showed up, trembling with fear because, should Jane find out, she would be beaten. Turned out a spy was at work, and true to the warning, Hajara was beaten.

"Who could beat a little girl?" Tom had to ask. But with the Martins on the ground, Hajara was sent to school the next day. She was petrified, shaking at being seen in the Martins' company. A bit of prodding brought out the story of another beating and another warning. To verify the story, Cheryl examined the girl, finding bruises and welts on her back and legs. Hajara told Cheryl of another day when she had been struck in the eye, and a neighbour took her to the hospital for treatment, where a nurse observed that the youngster had "the hands of an old woman."

"It won't happen again," the Martins pledged to each other. They appealed to the local chairman, a sort of mayor who deals with minor disputes in the neighbourhood — the Martins had sponsored a child or two of his to attend school — and he agreed to help.

"He knew us and our work; we were not stealing from the people. I asked him to go to Jane's house and get Hajara to collect her stuff — she only had a few clothes — and bring her to the school. We had already talked to a boarding school that we had helped, and they said they would take her in."

At the end of the school term, Hajara would be returned to her own family in another village.

Jane, the mistress, may have been dismayed when the Martins reported they had taken Hajara, but Tom and Cheryl were not deterred. "She was okay when we explained what we did," said Tom. "We have a good relationship with her. We still support her children. We tried to counsel her, because she didn't think she had done anything wrong. We even spoke to her minister, for all the good that did. It is a cultural thing."

The Martins talk about Hajara often, and with pride. In 2014, she was in Grade Nine, no longer fearful, but still with memories of her days as a house girl. When the Martins met her, her English was rudimentary, but, with their help and consistent school attendance, she turned into a good student with a solid grasp on English.

Hajara's story became a happy one, but the Martins encounter variations of her story regularly. Not all work out so successfully. Hajara's story is a common one in Uganda. Nearly ten years later, Tom writes about another girl whose story is virtually the same:

"We enrolled a new girl HCTH is sponsoring in Grade Eight today. She wrote a letter and told of working as a house girl and being beaten regularly for no reason. It is so sad. Thankfully she is away from that now. Her mother died in 2009 and she was living with an aunt. After school she had to look after cows, goats, dig in the garden, fetch wood, etc .... If the family felt she was too slow, she was beaten. She said she wants to be a nurse. She doesn't know when her birthday is."

Chapter 8
The Joy of Giving

"FROM WHAT WE GET WE MAKE A LIVING;
FROM WHAT WE GIVE, WE MAKE A LIFE."

— Arthur Ashe

"There is tremendous power and positive energy in giving — it is a shame that not enough people have experienced it to the fullest," says the introduction to the Pay It Forward Day website. It goes on to say that, at last count, more than 500,000 people in sixty countries around the world participated in Pay It Forward Day by making a positive difference in someone else's life.

The idea for a designated day sprang from a young adult novel called *Pay It Forward* written by Catherine Ryan Hyde and embraced by Australian Blake Beattie, who founded the Pay It Forward Day. Hyde builds her story around a Grade Eight student who was challenged by his social-studies teacher to do something that would change the world. His plan involved doing a good deed for three different people. The good deed came with a caveat that, rather than paying him back, the recipient would "pay it forward" to three others.

In practical terms, is it "more blessed to give than to receive?"

Scientists who have been studying the neuroscience of giving for several years say, "Yes." Among them is a team at the University of Oregon who scan brain patterns of volunteer subjects who consider give-or-not-give options. That team's work, along with many others', validates what Jesus told us centuries ago about the business of giving. It is a tenet held by many cultures and beliefs. We are hard-wired to be generous and are happiest when we are. By extension, it seems then, to be selfish means our wiring has gone amiss somewhere. The "me" generation might find an answer to many of its ills — ranging from the scramble for more to stepping on the backs of others to get ahead — by adjusting its motivation. (Altruists, researchers say, tend to age better and healthier than individuals without that characteristic.)

Somehow, the Martins have plugged into generosity in a way that not only attracts donors as partners but makes them feel personally connected with the individuals they help. At the same time, the Martins, and their donors, also experience the generosity of the people they meet, receiving gifts of fruit, invitations for meals, and items made especially for them. The recipients of aid are eager to give, even out of their poverty.

The International Director's Report is Tom's summary of the year's activities. It includes references to their diverse interactions with individuals and groups, but is weighted toward finance, since it is an accounting for donor gifts. It is as bare-bones as it is meticulous, and there's a story attached to virtually every line.

The tone was set with the first report in December, 2005.

On April 17, the Martins received a seventy-five dollar donation. It was the first of sixty days in which money arrived during the summer before they left for Peru. Exactly how much was not in the report, but Deb Neff's charity auction raised $5,300, and Bob Pringle and others donated items for a garage sale that realized $2,500.

As for how the money was used:

- Money was left in Peru to sponsor eight children and provide monthly support;
- Money was given to a single mother to start a hair salon in her home.— $2,500 for church construction was given to two congregations in Choma, Zambia;
- Money was given to buy chickens for a man in Zambia;
- Money was given to help a struggling pastor and teacher;
- $300 was given to buy Bibles in Uganda.

But none could match the catchy name of a new business started by four high school graduates in Uganda. *Radicals for Christ* received funds to purchase fifteen pigs.

The Martins took $5,000 to Peru in one of the early years, and the accounting revealed total expenditures of $4,993. What did they do with it? The Martins spent a bit of time in the historic city of Cusco, in the Andes, where they left $500 to buy food to be distributed in a hospital for the poor, a children's home, and a home for 110 blind children. In another community, they gave $500 to a clinic for malnourished babies, and $150 to buy food for a carpenter training program. Oher expenditures were outlined but there was no explanation for the remaining seven dollars, but postage would be a good guess.

In Lima's slum suburb of Manchay, the focus appears to have been buying school uniforms, paying tuition, and leaving enough cash to support eight students for ten months. They also donated funds to help repair fire damage to a home for twenty-five girls, enabled house mothers to buy clothes and Christian books in a children's' home, and to buy materials for a Bible Club.

One report talked about their early connections with a missionary family, who provided excellent accommodation for minimal rent. "Cheryl and I were amazed at how God worked things out in Peru, and He is still providing new contacts."

Then they went to Africa with $10,000. In Uganda, they worked with an Anglican minister whose charge included six prisons with inmates who needed "clothes and soap. Many had skin diseases and rarely got a decent meal. Some imprisoned mothers have their nursing babies with them."

They visited hospitals "and prayed for the sick, helping them with clothes, bed sheets, blankets, etc. [Many hospitals do not supply bed linens or, indeed, bed clothes for the patients.] The children's and maternity wards need baby clothes and teddy bears."

In Zambia, where the Martins had worked with Hope International, they simply picked up where they had left off. Money for church construction projects seemed to be major items, although "John wants chickens" was a notable entry. And they declared an interest in a Children's Home called "Children of the Most High," which wanted to start a church and school in a rural area.

Board Member Sterling DeWolfe and his wife, Faye, travelled to Zambia with the Martins on that early trip and took on that school as a personal mission of sorts, which we will discuss again later.

Scattered in the thick file of reports to the board are accounts of land or building purchases by Helping Cope Through Hope. One, in 2007, was for a HCTH mission house in Mityana, Uganda, $21,857.14. Broken down, the costs looked like this: initial purchase including legal and related charges, $16,083.53; water system and installation which included twenty men to put the tank in place, $1,442.35; electrical costs, $207.23; gate repair and locks, $261.47; security wall, $1,491.17; plumbing and eaves troughs, $221.17; clothes line, paint and tools, $47.00; truck rental, $108.82; fridge, stove with hook-ups, $914.70; furnishings, $1,079.70.

The following year, the board approved rental rates for missionaries staying for short periods: three hundred dollars a month or, for shorter periods, fifteen a night for singles, and twenty for couples. "The exception is the International Directors (Tom and Cheryl), who do not have to pay the monthly fee if they choose not to."

A housekeeping motion was also passed which required a two-thirds majority vote to approve the purchase or sale of any HCTH property or vehicles valued at more than $1,000. Then, in 2009, the board was told that a highlight was the purchase of land. In the next five years, three more parcels of land were acquired in Uganda and Zambia, where a growing number of families — nine at last count — were busy growing vegetables and raising poultry and livestock. Not only were they eating better, but, in some cases there has been enough of a surplus to sell.

The showpiece is in Zambia, where HCTH bought twelve hectares, one which many people have gardens or plots for livestock. Four houses, for four families, have been built.

Details of the agriculture activities are discussed later.

A regular problem is how to match budget demands with available funds. Financial advisors the world over repeat the same message: make a budget and stick to it. But when every day brings new situations that cry out for cash, that is a dilemma for Tom and Cheryl, who administer a blend of designated and discretionary funds. Those terms do not pop up in their lexicon, and the notion of a budget, in conventional terms, is simply the amount of money they have to spend.

Tom reported January 20, 2014:

"...there is too much work to do ... today we left home before eight thirty a.m. so that I could go to the bank [to withdraw money] ... I used it all today."

Then, he spills into an accounting of where the money went, the cows and pigs they bought, the school fees paid, food delivered. Every snippet includes thanks to a donor, mostly identified as a friend, a man from Canada, a ladies group, and, occasionally, an individual by name.

Another day, another report:

"I ran out of money today."

Supporters visiting the field see first-hand the way funds melt away. All seem to deal with a degree of guilt should they go home with any money left in their pockets.

One of the photographs illustrating the Martins' work on the ground shows two young men holding sieves they made to sell to carpenters for construction projects. Those sieves could be a metaphor for the distribution of HCTH funds to children, families, and the destitute who cross the Martins' path. They set out with pockets of cash —close to $120,000 in 2014 — for their three countries of service, knowing who-knows-what they'll find or how it will be spent.

A month later in March, another email reports:

"Money was given to Joel to build ten more desks for Lugwasyo school. ... we have decided to build another small house for a family whose house is falling down ... we also gave money to a lady to start a business [the money was given by a family in Canada]. We will probably leave one of our bicycles for her. She will buy cloth in Lusaka at twenty-five kwatcha and sell it for forty kwatcha in nearby villages."

Emails describe their trips to the market where they are enthusiastically welcomed, as is their money. Sometimes, the trip is to load up with foodstuffs to be doled out. Often, it is a report of Cheryl taking a youngster to buy school supplies and clothes. Those shopping expeditions with children might end up at a pizza or hamburger place, a new experience for kids who have rarely seen a real restaurant, much less ever gone inside.

In each country, the Martins have agents to represent them, distributing money on a systematic basis for school expenses or food to needy households when the Martins are out of the country. In Zambia, the local chairman gives money for food to eight or nine families; in Peru, money for school fees is paid to the school or responsible parents by the Martins' local representative, while in Uganda, Joram carries out HCTH assignments.

Gift certificates have become increasingly popular. In the first flurry of emails from Zambia in January, 2015, Tom reported about purchases made as a result of gift certificates:

"Beauty got a school bag, school shoes and socks, four skirts, and five blouses; Brian got a mattress and some pots. Others received bedding, plus goats and Bible."

Then, there are the flat-out cash donations with no strings attached. It is never hard to find a deserving destination.

Chapter 9
Donations

"AS WE HAVE OPPORTUNITY, LET
US DO GOOD TO ALL."

— Galatians 6:10 (NIV)

Canadians donated $10.6 billion to charity in 2010, only slightly higher than had been given three years earlier, according to a Statistics Canada article written by Martin Turcotte and based on the Canada Survey of Giving, Volunteering and Participating. The average annual donation was $114, down from $119 in 2007. Ninety-three percent of people described as religiously active (involved in a religious activity weekly) donated an average amount of $1,004 to charity; among those less active religiously, 83 percent donated an average of $313.

Religiously active people gave 40 percent of the total donations in 2010, of which 71 percent was given to religious organizations. Interestingly, only 27 percent felt motivated by religious obligations, while 89 percent were driven by compassion, a feature highlighted in the preamble to the Helping Cope through Hope constitution.

Arguably, there's a vast difference between selling and providing an opportunity. The Martins illustrate, in a

wonderfully benign way, how selling an opportunity works in the
HCTH universe. And they'd argue that it isn't selling at all. They
talk and they tell stories. Everywhere — in public gatherings,
in aeroplanes; in a walk in the park, or at the morning coffee
klatch — everybody is fair game for an introduction to HCTH.
In the historic Westport Knox Presbyterian Church, with its
160 years of supporting denominational and other missions,
about forty or so people gathered to listen to the Martin story.

As usual, it was a low key, casual event. A local supporter lent
the computer; the Baptist church, where the Martins had held a
meeting the previous year, lent the projector for the slide show;
a parishioner lent her nine-year old daughter, Zoe, the only
person present under the age of forty, as a technological advisor.
A clutch of woman crowded around a table where Cheryl had
baskets and jewellery for sale.

Tom's gift with kids was quickly demonstrated as a timid Zoe
turned into a confident assistant in a blink with Tom's whispered
guidance followed by a generous smattering of praise.

They didn't really need an introduction. Hugs and
handshakes from cousins and long-lost connections had already
occurred. "She went to school here, down the road toward
Newboro," "They had a farm…" etc.

A couple of weeks later, on a Sunday morning, the venue
changed, but only slightly. This time, it was the United Church
in Selby, Ontario, just north of Napanee. About thirty people,
middle-aged to seniors, drifted into the church basement. The
sanctuary, about as old as Knox in Westport, was locked due to
lack of business in the summer months, and the minister was
on vacation. It was all a good fit, and, true to form, the Martins
recognized both the need and opportunity. They could provide
the morning service and tell their story at the same time.
Besides, they were among friends again, including some who
had gone with them to Peru a year earlier.

The two old North American churches offered a subtle
juxtaposition to how the Martins describe many mission
churches. The rich oak wainscoting in Westport, the stained
glass windows, grand piano and organ, ceiling fans and

temperature control wrap parishioners in the warmth of time-honoured curved oak pews. To a Canadian audience, it looks like a church and smells like a church, where even the church mice are reverent.

In the slums of Zambia and Uganda, the churches are unadorned and stark. Better, maybe, than most of the dwellings of the parishioners, but practical as they are simple. Tom describes the flapping tarpaulin shielding worshippers from the sun and rain in one church with roughly hewn pews and barren walls. Any discomfort was overshadowed by the enthusiastic worship of the congregation which was jammed into space built to accommodate about half of them.

Though to be sure, in many urban African areas, churches often dominate their surroundings, impressive places in downtrodden neighbourhoods. In Nairobi, for instance, there is an abundance of great, beautiful churches just blocks from slums so desperate that even the air hangs heavy. And in Soweto, South Africa, in the whitewashed walls of the imposing church where Freedom fighters took refuge, bullet holes remain unpatched fifty years later. Now virtually a shrine.

The contrast between the spartan missions and the Canadian churches seemed appropriate, too, in reflecting the flavour of the Martins' public presentations that differ sharply from many religious — and secular — accounts of work among the poor and disadvantaged. The Martins simply recount events and describe individuals to illustrate what they do and how they do it. No hard sell for cash; the circumstances are just part of the fabric.

In explaining, Tom casually mentions how much it costs to be a sponsor for a child in school or university, or to buy gift certificates, or to provide any amount to be used as the Martins see fit.

It makes little difference whether it is a Sunday morning church service, mid-week church-sponsored meeting, or a community gathering; the pattern rarely varies. Through descriptions and photos, listeners are introduced to individuals — children, parents, and families — in far-off places, their lives, and what the Martins bring to them. Sprinkled along the way are asides, charming insights into their own lives and experience.

Watching Tom and Cheryl in their presentations is a study in salesmanship, group psychology, and marketing. And the most interesting part of it is that it is so natural that it is unlikely that they even recognize their own talent. If pressed, they'd protest that they are just humble people, and whatever good there is in their pitches comes from the hand of God.

Well, any churchman would say God uses many hands in many ways, and he gave the Martins a handful of talent. They invite their listeners simply to walk with them through their days.

In Zambia, the Martins have a 1950s Maytag washing machine, "a blessing for Cheryl." It does not have a wringer. In Uganda, she washes clothes by hand, which is "good exercise," according to Tom. He also says the days are so hot, and the roads so dusty, that a body wash is essential each night. Cheryl has a cold shower, but Tom's "bath" involves a basin of warm water from the rain barrel. Either way, cleaning up after a day in the heat and in the clouds of red dust, is a welcome respite before the visitors begin appearing at their home.

The dust gives way to mud when the rains come, a blessing after days of 36-degree weather that parches roads and fields — "it is nice to see our water tanks overflowing." Tom buys himself rubber boots. A youngster who walks for the better part of an hour to school gets a raincoat and umbrella.

A few in the audience shift with discomfort, visualizing the two orphans, maybe seven and eight, who had been abandoned on the street because their caregivers just "didn't want them anymore." The Martins did. He moves on to describe the environment that catches many of the little girls the Martins don't reach: they are offered a "home" in exchange for work. Usually hard work, with physical and sexual abuse included in the package.

Orphans — and there are many — are worst off, but destitute families also farm out their children, again mostly girls, because there isn't enough food to go around. Never mind the jammed hovels — the Martins never speak disparagingly about accommodation, always "homes," where a parent might sleep in a makeshift bed with three or four children, while the others — the numbers vary but mostly several — make do on the dirt floor.

It is all matter-of-fact descriptions of situations they see every day, such as visiting a handicapped grandmother who is raising seven children. Edward was one of those children. "When he was a baby, his father dropped him off and has not been seen since. They have no idea about his mother." The grandmother has been caught up in the HCTH approach, where the Martins do whatever it takes to relieve a burden.

They delivered maize flour, took the children to market, sponsored some in school, and, because the sponsors sent extra money, bought three goats and a pig for them. A Canadian woman earmarked a donation so that the grandmother, who has difficulty walking, could take a motorcycle taxi to church each week.

AIDS has ravaged Uganda, leaving thousands of orphans and widows among the victims to fend for themselves. In one school visited by Tom, he asked about their family units. Of the 250 students, about one hundred had no parents, another one hundred had one parent. Only fifty hands went up for having both a mother and a father.

The downstream effects of AIDS are illustrated by the example of one grandmother who had lost five children to the disease, leaving her with nineteen grandchildren, of which three quarters have AIDS themselves. "She is responsible to feed them all." Her home has become a haven for other orphaned or abandoned children as well, now spawning an orphanage for fifty and a school for about four hundred. A British charity gives her some support, and HCTH contributes to school fees since the students cannot pay them.

Uganda's AIDS epidemic surfaced in the early 1980s. By mid-decade, 30 percent of the country's population was living with AIDS, and President Museveni ordered a massive campaign: "abstain, be careful, use condoms." Support systems were implemented, and the incidence dropped to 6.4 percent of the population in 2006. Since 2011, however, Uganda is one of only three African countries where the incidence is increasing again. And, again, women are most vulnerable, due to their early marriages and the sexual activity frequently forced on them.

Tom tells about a girl named Brendah in Zambia. The Martins paid her school fees, even though she had failed the national Grade Seven exams twice. "The school accepted her because she was vulnerable. Her polygamist father had already sold two daughters into marriage, and, if Brendah was not going to school, she would suffer the same fate."

Another family they help had a fourteen-year-old daughter who is pregnant.

Tom slides effortlessly from one story to another. It fits — an easy style that goes with his extremely casual attire as opposed to a suit and shiny shoes. "People ask if I know in advance what I'm going to say. The answer is no; I just want to tell [people] what we've been doing."

Words tumble out, sometimes in disparate thoughts that leave listeners scratching their heads as he relates a story filled with "I said" and "he said." He has so much to tell in every story. He leans forward, smiling and stumbling over his words, punctuated with a bevy of "and so on"-s, and "anyways," before giving way to Cheryl, standing to his left, watching attentively, ready to jump in on cue.

"Cheryl, tell 'em…"

Sometimes, however, she needs no prompting. They were talking about an Ottawa woman and her thirteen-year-old daughter who visited them in Lima.

Tom: "It's kinda neat. People can stay with us."
Cheryl: "Four bedrooms."
Tom: "Yes."
Cheryl: "Each has a bathroom. There is a small kitchen."
Tom: "Cheryl cooks."
Cheryl: "We rent an apartment."
Tom: "From Kid's Alive. The airport can be intimidating."
Cheryl: "It's all Spanish."

Tom: "The bus station in Zambia is a terrible place."

As they go along, they make reference to how the money provided by supporters gets translated into school fees, food, bedding, and medicine. That's the closest they get to asking for money. They have about 350 regular supporters — "the number is growing a lot" — sponsoring more than 160 children, as well as building houses (fifteen by 2015), aiding several churches, and helping to start businesses or providing community facilities, such as latrines. Requests for HCTH to build outhouses are common, often along with the explanation that the petitioner "never had one."

Sanitation problems abound in all the countries, but are most daunting in Uganda, which is why Cheryl explained that getting a plastic bucket in their first home was "the height of luxury."

Given the age of the audience, they understood "night time walks" and tittered sympathetically. It also set Tom off on a riff about their first visit to an orphanage in the area where they are now working. It was 2005, and they had to walk across a courtyard among the goats and cows to reach their accommodation. No water or electricity, but lots of mosquitoes and an outhouse. Water hauled by the bucket meant an "African bath" — water in a basin.

The orphanage director offered to have the cook wash him. Tom passed.

Just a hesitation as the image soaked in, and Tom was back on track, talking about singing by lantern light with the forty or so children. One was a girl named Rachel, just one of the kids in the crowd. Seven years later, the Martins were at the secondary school paying fees when Rachel ran up and said, "You don`t remember me."

They didn't, but they do now. She had been in Grade Eleven when she got pregnant and lost her sponsorship. Another missionary paid for her twelfth year. But there was no available help for this brand new mother for Grade Thirteen.

"You can`t leave a child just a year short of graduation," The Martins had agreed, scrounging for the few dollars needed to help her graduate and, in the process, also found a sponsor for her son.

The story didn't end there, though. Rachel now had a shop and sold used clothes. At work, she befriended a young boy who was living on the street. He was hungry, unwell, and friendless. Samuel was seven when he traded the beatings he got at home for the insecurity of the streets. The streets were kinder. How he lived, what he ate, and where he slept for the next seven years are experiences that are forever locked in his memory, but a ray of sunshine appeared in the form of Rachel.

She allowed Samuel to sleep on a mattress on the floor of her rented one-room home on the nights when he didn't hang out overnight with the other street boys. Then, she got so broke that she had to sell her spare mattress. That left Rachel and her infant son to share the only mattress. One pillow, one sheet and one blanket. Samuel was left to sleep on the ground outside with mosquitoes for company.

Since the Martins had embraced Rachel in their network, her first thoughts turned to them when Samuel became ill. Malaria. She phoned, asking the Martins to meet her at the hospital.

In some ways, it is hard to say which is the lesser of the evils: malaria or the hospital. The waiting room was overflowing with mothers tending very sick children. Chickens wandered in and out. It was a dreary place. It still is. Incredibly, some people still manage to come out healthier than they went in, thanks to the excellent doctors who would do well in military field hospitals.

On seeing it, Cheryl cast a critical eye around and opined, "You wouldn't want to go there."

But Samuel did. He was sick, very sick, in his ragged pants and shirt, lying on a bare mattress without a sheet. Amid the scramble to provide him with some basic needs, Tom mentioned Samuel's plight in his email home. A Canadian responded, offering to help, which set the Martins off on a shopping expedition after observing, "That's how fast God works."

Among the purchases, in addition to clothes, was a mattress, so that he could sleep inside when he was discharged from the hospital. On it would be sheets brought from Canada, along with a pillow and blanket. Perhaps best of all was the mosquito netting, and the bonus was a toothbrush and paste.

Tom soon reported that Samuel looked better.

Hospitals figure infrequently in the Martin reports. They took some juice to Hassan, delivered some rubber gloves to Olivia who has a medical clinic, accompanied various girls to hospital for medication.

The Martins found Hassan when he was about four, malnourished, neglected, and left to die. They scooped him up, assisting and underwriting costs of medical help over more than seven years.

"His background has obviously affected him, as he now is eleven, but still in kindergarten class. He is not very big, either. He looks about five years old. He is a beautiful child of God, however."

Then there is Eddie. He is three, going on four, and hangs around the internet shop of the Martins' local representative, Joram. Tom describes him as a "cute little guy" whose sister works nearby. His mother brews beer in the village and is rarely around, so he's left to his own devices.

"One night, his sister left her work and never picked Eddie up, so Joram brought him home to the house he shares with the Martins. The next morning, the Martins allowed Eddie to sleep until eight when he needed to go to school. After classes, which end at one p.m., Cheryl took him to the market to get him shoes, socks, underwear, shirts, shorts, and three small toys. Joram had explained that Eddie really had no clothes of his own; what he wore was borrowed from another child. He wanted to wear his new wardrobe right away.

He was lonely, missing his father and not quite understanding that his Dad would never come back. The father had died in a freak accident when a tree branch fell on him.

These stories had the audiences riveted, itching to help. A few wrote cheques. At the end of the presentations, attention shifted to a table of scarves, artwork, and hats brought from the field. While the folks milled about, the Presbyterian Women's Guild at Knox plied them with cakes, squares and cookies.

At the United Church presentation, a talented pianist — who was filling in for vacationing staff — offered lively versions of old gospel favourites. Tom switched on his microphone — he had been told in Westport a couple of weeks earlier that age was taking its toll on the hearing of his typically small audiences. He announced the opening hymn, but here the hearing disconnect was with the pianist. He began to play, Tom began to sing. Different hymns. It took a couple of bars and a restart before an unflustered Tom got everyone onto the same page before moving on to a scripture text from Isaiah in which God asks, "Whom shall I send," and Isaiah responded "Here I am, send me." It fits. He also used the opportunity to acknowledge several people in the audience, naming them, and mentioning how many children they had sponsored. The congregation itself was sponsoring a child.

It was a warm and friendly group, responsive to Tom's suggestion that they sing some songs popular among the children in Africa. Cheryl held up a poster-sized sheet with the words of a song, and Tom invited the audience to sing along. "He is the Lord of the sky. He is the Lord of the sea. He is the Lord of you. He is the Lord of me. He has forgiven my sins. He has set me free. He is Lord of all."

There were more verses and his audience of mostly seniors responded, first tentatively and then lustily, as they recalled their Sunday School days. Tom moved on. "Here's another kind of cute tune. Remember Puff the Magic Dragon? Well, that's the tune but different words. "God's Love is like a circle, a circle big and round..."

Like kids everywhere, African youngsters quickly seize the catchy tunes. And while Tom focuses on the messages in the choruses, the kids are "really learning English, which is a side benefit, I suppose...."

Chapter 10
Pop Cans to University

"CAN YOU HELP?"
— An information sheet prepared by the DeWolfes

Every Wednesday, Faye and Sterling DeWolfe haul a trailer filled to overflowing with aluminum cans they've collected to a local recycling plant. They unload it and head home with somewhere between $80 and $120. Sterling's little notebook tracks every dollar they get, and it's all for Zambian projects, augmented with a sizeable chunk of their personal pensions.

They are long-time friends of Tom and Cheryl Martin. The men taught school together, the women both worked in health care and raised families. They attended the same church. As often occurs, their lives took different paths but periodically intersected, which is what happened when Tom retired from teaching. Their shared passion for helping others — especially children — brought them together again.

When Sterling reconstructed this history for me, he sounded every bit like an elementary school teacher, speaking slowly and enunciating every word. "We [Faye and Sterling] have been on many mission endeavours with several different organizations, and the Martins said they wanted to do something similar, ministering to people, mainly children."

They discussed their desire to help educate children and to improve their lives, first on a trip to Hawaii together, and many times later at each other's homes.

"Tom had a vision and I agreed with what he wanted to do. He asked if I would serve on the board, and I said 'Well, if you think I can help, yes.'"

Sterling became one of the founding directors of Helping Cope Through Hope. With Faye, he also embraced the concept embedded in the HCTH constitution of visiting the sites of HCTH endeavours. It is in Zambia where their personal interventions with HCTH have had the greatest impact.

Which project dominates? Hard to say. Maybe the school in the wilderness that now has a latrine for the impoverished students as well as blackboards, tables, and chairs. Or maybe the farm carved out of barren land with its elevated water tank, gardens, pig pen, and an incubator for chicks. Or maybe it's the girl they sponsored and shepherded through school to the doors of a university, although sadly, this story took a disappointing turn.

On their first visit to Zambia, they cemented their relationship with a local church, as well. Tom's email reported that Sterling "had a very effective ministry on Friday and Saturday. He preached on Sunday and fifteen came forward for prayer and to accept Jesus Christ." Faye told the Easter story in Junior Church, which was attended by more than two hundred.

As the two couples chatted with the pastor and friends on the church steps, "a fairly large snake" — a dangerous Eel — was crawling near the door. The pastor interrupted his description of a poor mission school in the country to dispatch the snake with a brick. A few days earlier, there was another snake encounter — a cobra. This time, the snake and the Martins came to an understanding — they would go their separate ways.

Snakes may have attracted their attention, but it was a school that really seized their interest. It was about ninety minutes into the desolate hinterland, far from the slums on the outskirts of

Choma where HCTH was most active. The Shalom Community School, along with an orphanage, was run by an organization called Children of the Most High. The descriptions they heard strained credibility.

"So, me, being a retired teacher..." Sterling recalled "That sounds interesting, let's go."

The prospect of a dusty dirt road with an abundance of ruts and potholes didn't faze them; they had already experienced the four-hour rough ride over 285 kilometres by bus from Lusaka, the Zambian capital, to Choma, so this wasn't much of a challenge. They had done it all before, having visited many church-based mission projects in underdeveloped countries, partly as adventures, and partly as an opportunity to serve.

It was 2006 when they first laid eyes on the beautiful school building, clearly out of place with its steel roof and concrete block walls. Americans had donated the funds for the building's shell, and that's as far as the money had gone. Inside, about 350 kids sat on logs resting on bricks, or on the floor, in four classrooms. There was one decrepit blackboard and no chalk. Primitive by even Zambian standards, it catered to children who were too poor to attend the government-sanctioned schools because they lacked pretty much everything — no shoes, no uniforms, no supplies, and not much of a future.

In December, 2014, a United Nations Children's Fund reported that 25 percent of the basic Zambian schools were without safe water and had limited toilet facilities, up to one toilet for 124 students compared with a desired ratio of one toilet for twenty-five girls or forty boys. In about 2012, the school was threatened with closure if it didn't have latrines. The de Wolfe's aluminum cans project solved that problem at The Children of the Most High School. It now has covered latrines for boys and girls, a luxury.

Nearly half of Zambia's 14 million people (2012) live in the cities and, economically, it is making progress, but rural areas are sparsely populated by mostly subsistence farmers. The area around Choma, is one of those areas. The people scratch out a meagre existence, stretching their capacity to provide the essentials of life for the typically large families. Seventy-eight percent live below the recognized poverty line. So, even though basic education for years one to nine — which is considered a decent level of education — is mandated, circumstances can be extremely primitive if children manage to go to school at all. UNESCO (United Nations Educational, Scientific and Cultural Organization) estimated that 80 percent of primary school age children were enrolled in school in 2002. It did not measure quality.

Choma, population 40,000, is a market town and the commercial hub of the province. To the children attending the Shalom Community School, it is a world they didn't know.

"Our hearts were heavy," the DeWolfes recounted as they surveyed the surroundings on their first visit and the youngsters with big, round eyes looking back at them. White folks weren't all that common to them, just as the woebegone skeleton of a school was unfamiliar to the DeWolfes.

The retired teacher, who was sixty-seven at the time with more than thirty years among elementary school students, barely hesitated: "Give us a list of all the items needed to complete the school and the cost of each."

The information became the backbone of a simple brochure called *Can You Help?* which they made and handed out at church, to friends, and to businesses when they got home. *Can You Help?* listed the costs of materials the school owners, or the DeWolfes themselves, identified as needed. $106 for a window frame, $1 for door hinges, $15.50 for five litres of paint and $3.50 for a brush to apply it. Then there were the teaching tools, $192 for a student's desk, $207 for a teacher's table and chair, $45 for a chalkboard.

Simple but effective, the brochure attracted $8,000 in donations in six months as well as the attention of DeWolfes' grandchildren.

"Could we help collecting cans?" they asked. With the re-cycling plant in the DeWolfes' home town of Napanee, it was a no-brainer. The grandparents, however, drew the line at patrolling highways with green garbage bags. Should someone else gather cans from the ditches and deliver them to their garage, the DeWolfes would be grateful.

Another simple promotion piece, this time a poster. "Help your pop cans make a big difference. Help us educate needy children in Africa." Their efforts made a newspaper feature and drew cans. Local churches and businesses began saving them, and individuals left bags on the DeWolfes' doorstep. The grandchildren collected cans in their town a few miles from Napanee. Each week, the mounds on their trailer strain at the straps and tie-downs that crisscross it.

Over time, the DeWolfes' projects generate an average of about $2,500 a year for supplies, the library, and an annual stipend — though it isn't much — for the teachers.

An email (March, 2014) from Tom reported that they had paid school fees for several students, all with money realized by the DeWolfes' recycled cans. But their impact on HCTH work in Zambia reaches much farther. Its breadth surfaces from other sources, including their involvement on the eight-hectare farm called Esperanza, meaning Hope, just outside Choma.

The Martins bought the raw land as a way of helping some poverty-stricken slum dwellers achieve a degree of self-sufficiency. The DeWolfes joined in, shoulder-to-shoulder, in turning the fertile soil into a maturing mixed farming operation. They underwrote the cost of barns, financed and designed an irrigation system and a chicken incubator warmed with solar panels. A fish pond was a 2014-15 addition.

Some of this work coincided with the DeWolfes' fourth visit to Zambia, which, they said, may be their last. Malaria had caught them both and laid them flat. Sterling was so sick that, at his final doctor's visit, the doctor comforted him by saying not to worry about the bill until he was feeling better. It was about fifty dollars. Paying the bill was less of a struggle for the still-recovering couple than the thirty-two-hour voyage home to Canada.

"I don't think we can [visit Zambia] again," Faye says, and quickly adds, "But we could go back to Peru."

They have left their footprint, however, in Africa. A farming report from the Primach Hope Rehabilitation project on the last quarter of 2014 acknowledged the extensive participation of both the Martins (through HCTH) and the DeWolfes: It mentioned several projects, highlighting the purchase of two incubators and the sponsorship of most of the kids into school this year. (In January, 2015, one of the new incubators received its first eighty-four eggs with an anticipated hatch date twenty-seven days later.

On their first visit to Zambia, the DeWolfes met Precious, fourteen, and her sister, Esther, sixteen. The girls lived in a compound called Mwapona, across a marsh on a dusty — or muddy — country road from Choma. Tiny houses there are jammed together. The air is acrid with the smoke from outdoor fires cooking meals built around the Zambian staple of maize.

This was the settlement to which the Martins led their friends when they offered to extend their commitment to sponsoring needy children. The Martins had jumped at a possible fit. To make the introductions, they walked through the fields and low-lying marshy areas to a cramped and tiny home for the meeting. A family of eight lived there — the parents, both HIV positive, and six children. The older girls, Esther and Precious, were the kids the Martins had in mind. They had potential, but found it difficult to go to school because they had to look after the younger children. The mother, said Faye, was very ill. The father, like many of the men in the town, did odd jobs, but was mostly idle.

"The home was very small, bricks and mud, with a thatched roof, a gravel floor, with two mattress-sized bedrooms. The parents had a mattress, the kids slept on the floor. Just a place to sleep inside, and then they cooked outside. That's where we met the girls."

"What did they look like?" I asked.

"Want to see a picture?"

"Why don't you just tell me?"

There was a longish pause as Sterling pondered an appropriate answer. "Well, they were black."

Faye helped out: "Precious now is tall, quite beautiful, keeps herself looking attractive. We were just attracted to them. They were dressed as well as could be expected; they weren't in rags."

Then, with still a touch of disbelief, Faye added, "And [Precious] washed my feet!" Faye had been wearing rubber thongs on the trip through the marsh.

What North American would not be moved by a fourteen-year-old kid who spontaneously made such a gesture? Looking down on the rich, shiny black hair of Precious, Faye's thoughts may have been carried back to another era in Biblical times when foot washing was a normal thing, often with an extraordinary, hidden meaning. Down there at toe-level, it would be a sign of humility and respect, heaping honour on the guest.

The DeWolfes were smitten. If the girls were willing to work hard and achieved good marks, their education would be assured. In telling the story, the focus from the outset was Precious, with Esther playing second fiddle. The reason became apparent as the story unfolded.

It wasn't always smooth sailing with either girl. Precious needed both encouragement and prodding, just like the Canadian youngsters with whom Sterling had spent a lifetime. Sensitivity and affection, through visits in 2008 and 2010 — they tried writing, but that didn't work — were required as Precious moved through secondary school. It was difficult to keep Precious in school, and it required several interventions, including arranging for Precious to change schools to keep her plugging along.

It wasn't a lack of interest alone that impeded her progress. Part of the problem was her mother's illness — she needed Precious at home.

"She took on the mother's role. So we said that if she graduated from high school, we would pay for her to attend university," said Sterling. In university, she'd learn important social skills, how to manage money and time, and of course, a degree.

One could sense the DeWolfe's feeling of accomplishment when they set out for Zambia in 2014, loaded with all sorts of plans, to say nothing of money to pay her university tuition fees, buy her appropriate clothing, and arrange accommodation. Such excitement when they arrived. And then obstacles appeared. Precious didn't have her high school transcript; she had given it to an intermediary. The reason was unclear. However, Precious needed it in hand to be accepted at the university.

Sterling talked to the mystery intermediary, who said she had the transcript and agreed to meet them in Lusaka, where the university was located. The plans were firm, but the intermediary wasn't. She didn't show, and then, inexplicably, was unreachable. Equally unreachable on short notice was a copy of the transcript. Apparently, it was in the hands of government officials in yet another city. But the DeWolfes had run out of time.

They went home with the hope that, when the Martins returned to Zambia in 2015, they would be able to gather up the pieces. There was just a hint of despair when Sterling talked about university, saying costs could have been shaved had Precious applied for grants and bursaries, "but she didn't." He hastened to add: "We haven't given up on her yet."

"We will pay her tuition and room and board — if she goes. The deal was 'finish your school and don't get pregnant.' So many girls at her age get pregnant, and we told her she needed to be careful not to be saddled with a child."

Was their intervention a success? A pause and, in unison, "Yes. Look how far she has come, and we are looking at another university, sponsored by the Free Methodist Church. We just talked to them last week." They warmed to the idea, because this institution is a live-in university, where Precious would not encounter as many difficulties.

The trouble was that when the Martins returned to Zambia, the bitter truth became apparent. Precious had not been in school as she'd said she had been, and thus, there was no transcript. At the time of writing, her future with the DeWolfes and the Martins was in doubt.

Esther, on the other hand, had fallen by the wayside early on. Drugs got her, and obviously it saddened them, but their account is equally without rancor. Just the facts.

"Esther wasn't truthful. She'd say she was going to school, but she wasn't. She wasn't living at home; she was into drugs and was pregnant. We told her our purpose was to educate her, and she didn't or wouldn't help.

"We still care for her and her baby. We see her, but all she wants is money."

Are they disappointed? Yes. Are they chagrined or disillusioned? No. The ebb and flow of helping the disadvantaged is part of the calling. Their Zambian efforts focused on two young women, who, they believed, only needed a hand to get ahead. They had done what they could.

At home, in Napanee, they met another challenge, testimony to their determination, their commitment, and their deep-seated faith.

Her name is Justine. She was twenty-two, living on the street, when the DeWolfes found her in 2006. An orphan, she had been given up for adoption when she was three with cigarette burns all over her body. She was adopted, but, when she was eleven, she became a government ward, living in a series of group homes. She had a child and was deemed incapable of caring for it.

"She had a lot of hurts and abandonments," said the DeWolfes who became the closest thing she had to family. Sterling recalls getting the phone call many parents receive from children: she was miles away with no money and had been abandoned again. They arranged bus fare to bring her home.

Then, she met a man, lived with him for a year, became pregnant, and had a child who died. The father refused to allow her to see the deceased infant and had it cremated without her knowledge. The couple fought, she was convicted of assault and ultimately sent to a federal penitentiary.

Due to her emotional instability she bounced from one penitentiary to another before landing in Saskatoon, Saskatchewan, miles and miles from Napanee, where her behaviour resulted in segregation for days at a time, tied up and unable to go to the bathroom for many hours. Her sentence kept getting extended because of her aggression.

"It was all she could do," said Faye. "They didn't know how to treat her. They treated her roughly, and she responded in the only way she could."

News reports during this period recounted the story of another disturbed young woman abused in the Canadian penitentiary system who committed suicide while guards watched.

"We said that if we don't step in, Justine could do the same thing."

They flew to Saskatoon, four hours away by plane, to work on her behalf in co-operation with Elizabeth Fry officials and others, who hastened her release from prison.

"We are continuing to support her. She calls us Mom and Dad. She phones... not every day, but regularly. She's making great progress. She's not cutting herself any more, not running to the emergency wing of the hospital, and has an apartment of her own.

"We're encouraging her to make better choices." Their intervention became a segment in a national television documentary.

If the Zambian sisters could only see themselves in the Canadian girl's mirror, they'd find the same sort of unconditional love. In the meantime, the DeWolfes are leaving it "in God's hands."

Chapter 11
The Mission Landscape

"CHRISTIANITY, COMMERCE AND CIVILIZATION."
— David Livingstone

Two explorers with diametrically different objectives and faiths blazed the trails that the Martins have been travelling with their own set of imperatives. David Livingstone, revered in the English-speaking world, was first an explorer and then a missionary wandering through what now includes Uganda and Zambia. Francisco Pizarro, a Spanish conquistador was busy in South America much earlier, spreading misery and disease along with the Catholic faith in Peru. On the plus side, he championed education. The influences of both still trickle through society, often unrecognized and unacknowledged.

It was Livingstone, the much-honoured and perhaps over-rated missionary-explorer, who was looking for the headwaters of the Nile River when he came upon Victoria Falls (he named it after Queen Victoria) and said, "Scenes so lovely must have been gazed upon by angels in flight."

It took years before the Martins took a break from their work to see those mighty falls, considered the largest in the world. Twice as wide and one and a half times as high as Niagara

Falls, it is the centre piece for the Victoria National Park, which abounds with wildlife, causing Tom to reflect that "God made some beautiful animals." And, while he didn't say so, their visits had to be tempered with a sadness that, in about 150 years, some things in Africa haven't changed all that much.

A statue of Livingstone stands at the base of the falls with the inscription: Christianity, Commerce and Civilization. Livingstone believed that these values would provide an alternative to the rampant slave trade and would give dignity to Africans. He was convinced that preaching the gospel and promoting economic improvements and social conditions were not mutually exclusive.

He preached a Christian message but did not force it on unwilling ears. At the same time, he was uncompromising in his faith. A journal entry gives insight into his spirituality: "I place no value on anything I have or may possess, except in relation to the kingdom of Christ. If any will advance the interests of the kingdom, it shalle (sic) be given away or kept, only as by giving or keeping it, I shall promote the glory of Him to whom I owe all my hopes in time and eternity."

He hated slavery and opposed it, while working closely with the locals to embrace education, health care, and Christianity. In many ways, his preoccupations could be as easily applied, in the present era, to the Martins and their approach to missionary work.

Livingstone was named among the one hundred Greatest Britons in a 2002 U.K-wide vote. He died in Zambia in 1873, and, despite his legacy as a missionary as well as an explorer, he only left one recorded convert behind: Sechele, a leader of an African tribe. Although Sechele was apparently a faithful Christian, some of his traditions and cultural heritage kept bubbling to the fore. He got rid of four of his five wives at Livingstone's insistence, but one of the abandoned wives became pregnant, and Sechele was the father. He also clung to the tradition of rainmaking, reported Neil Parsons of the University of Botswana.

In a BBC account (2013), Parsons suggested that Sechele "did more to propagate Christianity in nineteenth-century southern Africa than virtually any single European missionary." Not all missionaries agreed, their views influenced by his clinging to aspects of his cultural environment.

Other explorers looking for the source of the Nile also blazed the way for missionaries. Could it be, however, that Livingstone and Sechele laid the groundwork for Zambia's current situation? Protestants arrived in 1877 with the Catholics hot on their heels in 1879.

The 2002 census reported that more than 80 percent of the population was Christian and 12 percent were Muslim, with the rest spread over fringe groups including traditional religions. The percentages have not shifted much. Among the Christians, the Roman Catholic Church had 41.9 percent of the population among its adherents, the Anglican Church of Uganda had 35.9 percent, with Evangelical and Pentecostal groups making up most of the balance.

A text called *Studying Africa Through the Humanities* describes Africans as "notoriously religious," and another text describes how some Africans mix Christianity and traditional religion — the individual goes to church on Sunday and follows some elements of traditional African religion as well.

Christianity, however, is Zambia's official religion and is enshrined in the 1966 constitution. About 87 percent of the population is Christian, and Zambia has one of the largest Seventh Day Adventist concentrations in the world — one in eighteen claims attachment to the denomination.

There is a growing sentiment that Africa and South America are the new Christendom. Surveys suggest that, increasingly, North Americans are abandoning church and traditional religious beliefs. There also is a demographic shift underway as reported in a 2014 United Nations study. Africa had nine percent of the world's population in 1950 but will have more than forty percent by the end of the century. An estimated 1.8 billion babies will be born in Africa in the next thirty-five years, and 37 percent of the world's children will be African by 2050.

Much of that population boom will be in the poorest countries, with Niger having the highest fertility rate with an average of 7.5 children per woman.

While the countries that are served by the Martins do not match those birth rates, large families are the norm, and poverty afflicts vast numbers of their population. However, the potential for economic development is showing signs of shaking off a dormant history. How that plays out is a story still unfolding, but, in the meantime, the Martins are working to ensure more of the young people are not left standing on the sidelines.

Zambia and Uganda are neighbours, sharing parts of the Nile River basin. Exactly where the river rises on its way to becoming the most famous river in the world is somewhat imprecise. However, Uganda seems to have the lock on it and sits almost completely within its basin. Both benefit from its valuable attributes, including shipping capabilities.

UGANDA

Uganda's name appears not to have a precise meaning, but may have evolved from being part of the "Buganda Kingdom," which included a large portion of the southern part of the country. Bantu-speaking settlers drifted in from central Africa, bringing with them ironworking skills and new ideas for social and political organizations. It is the second most populous landlocked country in Africa, with an estimated 35,800,000 souls in 2012, and it is one of the poorest, despite a wealth of natural resources.

Uganda has also had more than its share of violence, aided by corruption, poverty, and international neglect, factors that are not reflected in national anthem, "Oh Uganda, Land of Beauty," which was adopted in 1962.

Oh Uganda! may God uphold thee,:We lay our future in thy hand.:United, free,:For liberty:Together we'll always stand.

Oh Uganda! the land of freedom.:Our love and labour we give,:And with neighbours all:At our country's call:In peace and friendship we'll live.

Oh Uganda! the land that feeds us:By sun and fertile soil grown.:For our own dear land,:We'll always stand::The Pearl of Africa's Crown.

The song rings with hope while championing friendship and the country's rich agricultural potential. It is a perspective that has been elusive in modern history, its landscape scarred by warfare and atrocities both within its borders and in adjoining countries.

Other countries, too, have stained histories, including Kenya to the east, South Sudan (and Somalia) to the north, Congo to the west, and Tanzania to the south. The current president, who came to power in a 1986 coup, has been embraced by the West, but his reputation was marred by his intrusion into the second Congolese war; the war in the Congo has resulted in an estimated 5.4 million deaths since 1998.

The number of internally displaced persons is estimated at 1.4 million.

Economically, Uganda has substantial natural resources including oil and gas. In 2008, Uganda recorded 7 percent growth, despite the world-wide economic downturn. However, despite improved economic conditions, more than 35 percent of the population lives on less than $1.25 a day. Most live in rural areas, which are home to 85 percent of the population. The nation's government loses an estimated $286 million a year to corruption.

Tom Martin doesn't appear to be deterred by history. Asked which mission field attracts him most, he pauses for only a second before stating, "Uganda is where my heart is." Cheryl isn't as definitive, saying her attachment is equal: "Wherever we are is where my heart is."

Tom sees only individuals scratching out an existence who can still laugh and love and share a bit of maize with two white foreigners who have moved in among them. They watch at first, eyes getting wide as the Martins embrace a whole family touched by illness or death. The trust builds. Tom said: "I never feel afraid. Our friends and neighbours say, 'we'll look after you'.

"We go to their homes. Whatever and wherever it is. It doesn't matter. We sit on their couch. It can be torn, ragged with springs sticking through. Even bugs. It doesn't matter.

"The poorest of the poor, those are the people we work with. They are like our own, our children and grandchildren. We know them by name. Even their birthdays." That is, for those who happen to know the date, or have picked a day and year for their birth to commemorate.

"How old are you? 13. . .maybe 14, maybe 15."

The fact that Tom is busy learning bits of a local language — Luganda — hastens acceptance when he tries out the words and phrases. Market merchants break into huge smiles when he asks "how much" in their local dialect.

Uganda's population is among the youngest in Africa (median age is fifteen) and its women are among the hardest working females, with an average workday of twelve plus hours, (compared with eight plus for men). Child labour is rife, abuse abounds, and life-threatening disease lurks everywhere. It is an overwhelming place, where making a difference seems an impossible task.

Tom made flying trips to Uganda in August, 2014 and 2015, to oversee the enrolment of several HCTH-sponsored students in university — a huge achievement in such a country. One graduate now is in the United States; two other students are in first year.

ZAMBIA

Zambia grew out of a tangled web of uprisings and territorial disputes that flared intermittently in the region from the days of the British South Africa Company and Cecil Rhodes (about 1888). With independence claimed on October 24, 1964,

Northern Rhodesia became the Republic of Zambia, taking its name from the Zambezi River, which means God's river. It sits between Mozambique and Angola, bounded in part by some of the major rivers that flow out of what is known as the Zambezi basin, which includes Victoria Falls.

The geography varies from broad flat plains in the north with a flood plain on the west — generally flooded November to April — and a hilly to mountainous region on the east. This diversity, which also features Kalambo Falls, Africa's second highest waterfall, gives Zambia a tropical climate which is less brutal than some neighbouring countries.

Sterling DeWolfe says he'd return to Zambia but not Uganda — "it's too hot." Zambia's average monthly temperature is about 20 degrees centigrade for upwards of eight months a year, with pleasant subtropical weather from May through August.

Sitting as it does among neighbours who are afflicted with an ongoing history of strife, Zambia has been a magnet for nearly 88,000 refugees and asylum seekers, according to a 2009 World Refugee Survey. They amount to almost 6 percent of the total population of 14 million. About 60,000 live in camps with the balance blended into local populations. If they want to work, they need a permit that costs up to five hundred dollars a year.

These beleaguered people contribute to the statistic that, between 2000 and 2010, showed 68 percent of the Zambian population lived in poverty — 78 percent in rural areas. Strife, home and abroad, also frustrates economic growth, because, given its inland location, the country relies heavily on transportation routes through other jurisdictions to get exports such as minerals to market.

The price of copper (Zambia's principal export) has shrunk for years, pushing Zambia into the cadre of the most heavily indebted countries in the world. A Global Competitiveness Index in 2007 ranked Zambia eleventh from the bottom. While there was good progress with mining activity and improved copper prices, which began turning around in about 2000, it all hit the skids in 2015. Weak copper prices and an electricity shortage "has put pressure on Zambia's mining industry," reported Reuters in September, "threatening output, jobs, and economic growth." The article listed major mining companies that may have to shut down some operations, prompting one analyst to say, "This is serious, it could bring our economy to its knees."

Agriculture, next to mining, is a key economic contributor, in part because of its labour intensity. For example, products ranging from various meats, dairy products, eggs to edible oils are the outputs of one company that employs 4,000 workers. In recent years, several hundred dispossessed white farmers left Zimbabwe to take up farming in Zambia at the invitation of the Zambian government.

Still, in 2010, the World Bank recognized Zambia as a pace-setter among economically reformed countries, even though it was battered by the 2009 world economic crisis. Now, its progress is being threatened again.

Lusaka, the capital, is one of the fastest growing cities in southern Africa with about 10 percent of the nation's population. It is located on a plateau in the south-central part of the country, where the nation's four major transportation corridors merge. Copperbelt Province in the northwest is the next most heavily populated area, with nearly half of its population living in urban centres. Understandably, the population tends to congregate along the transportation corridors with the tantalizing possibility of employment. There are not enough jobs to go around, and all share the problem of underemployment or unemployment, a plight that is expected to worsen.

Rural areas are home to mostly subsistence farmers, thinly spread out across the country.

Government-provided education, particularly in rural areas, is spotty and tuition is free only to year seven. Year nine is considered a decent level of education. Historically, the private school system was the purview of Christian missions and continues to be a cornerstone of many religious endeavours, such as HCTH. Public education, badly underfunded, is less desirable.

The Martins focus mainly on health and education matters in Zambia, leaning on native churches — most often Anglican or Catholic — for local intelligence and areas of need. In the early days, messages home focussed often on church activities, but the accounts have become more community oriented as the Martins' efforts target areas where the perceived need is greatest. One of Tom's early emails described a church service in which the Martins and DeWolfes participated. About 200 children were in attendance "in a church twenty feet by twenty feet. You can see why we brought money to build a new church." Those available funds had the locals working on trusses within a week.

Tom wrote: "Yesterday we went to visit Joseph. This is the man we gave the guitar to last year. We saw the new house he is building. HCTH gave him three hundred dollars to build the house."

At first blush, a guitar from Canada seems an unusual addition to the bags of clothes the Martins take (and wear) to the mission field. A Canadian, however, donated this guitar, autographed by entertainer Dan Akroyd, and another donor filled it with 1,500 suckers. It replaced a primitive guitar which Joseph had made himself.

Joseph's delight was at the sound, not the candy. The following year, the Martins brought new replacement strings and another guitar, this one fulfilling a longing expressed by a local pastor who, like his parishioners, financially lived on the edge.

"The pastor here was telling us he has seven children. His oldest son is in Lusaka, trying to earn money to go to college. He has been there four years. He is going to start attending part time, as it is cheaper. The pastor makes a salary of about sixty-five US per month. This is not enough to feed themselves properly, as food prices here are not much different than in Canada. In addition they have to pay school fees."

On another day, Tom asks supporters: "[A] little girl named Melody has a very large deformed upper lip. This causes her a lot of discomfort and hurt from other children. The doctors say it cannot be fixed, as it is too dangerous to operate. We are going to visit her and pray that God will heal her of this deformity. Would you please pray for Melody also that God would do what doctors say they can't. Thank you!"

PERU

The differences between the African countries and Peru are as profound as their histories and geography. Desert, rain forests, mountains, valleys, farming, and fishing are among the characteristics of this nation of 31 million along the Pacific Coast. Its people are industrious and proud of their history and the advances made in more recent times.

They are Mesoamericans, part of the ancient civilization of South America, and brothers of what ultimately became twelve independent countries: Argentina, Bolivia, Brazil, Chile, Colombia, Ecuador, Guyana, Paraguay, Peru, Suriname, Uruguay, and Venezuela. Whereas Africa became the hotbed of the slave traders and explorers, conquistadors from the time of Columbus came to South America with mainly looting on their mind, looking for wealth and territory to expand the reach of their host countries. Slavery appears to have been more of a by-product.

Francisco Pizarro was one of the conquistadors. His wanderings brought him to Peru in the 1520s where he planned to conquer the great empire of the Inca, a country renowned for its civilization. He swept through the nation, wiping out much of the population and plundering its gold, leaving behind new diseases and untold hardship.

Treachery, chicanery, and deceit were his trademarks. Hostility and distrust dogged his path. He did, however, found the first Spanish settlement at what became San Miguel de Piura and introduced Catholicism. Promoting Christianity, though, was not his long suit.

Pitched battles ensued, and the invaders destroyed the settlements of the Incas that had been developed with outstanding engineering feats over the previous three hundred years. Incan Emperor Atahualpa was captured in a battle in 1532 and, in an act of treachery that lives on in the minds and hearts of the indigenous people, was executed in 1533. Pizarro had demanded a room full of gold for the emperor's release, and when the treasure was delivered, he ordered the execution of the emperor anyway.

Partly in the name of the Catholic Church, native temples and settlements were destroyed as Pizarro extended his reach to the Incan capital of Cusco in the Andes highlands. But the Incas, with their skills and intelligence, resisted. Secretly, they blotted out all evidence of the routes leading to the most sacred site of their empire, Machu Picchu, which remains a monument to this day, and is recognized as one of the wonders of the world. It stands on a mountain top overlooking vast, thick jungles below, where it is thought other Inca treasures such as Machu Picchu may still lie undiscovered in forests virtually too thick to penetrate.

Thousands of visitors from around the world hike the Inca Trail to Machu Picchu, an arduous four-day trek from Cusco. Less hardy visitors take a four-hour train ride, saving their energy for the steep climbs over the mountain top to see up close the jaw-dropping result of feats, for example, of moving rocks weighing as much as one hundred tons up the mountain side. There are countless rocks like that, fitted together and terraced by skilled stone masons whose workmanship is still considered extraordinary. Seams between rocks have paper-thin tolerances. The rocks are so skillfully assembled that they have withstood up to a thousand years in one of the most earthquake-prone regions of the world.

The frequency and severity of the earthquakes make the architectural and engineering achievements of the Incas even more remarkable. In November, 2014, an earthquake measured 5.8 on the Richter Scale and was centred two hundred miles north of Lima. Damage at Machu Picchu was minimal, in sharp contrast to the widespread damage a devastating earthquake caused two years earlier in nearby Chile.

Thwarted in the north by the canny natives, Pizarro turned his attention south and founded Lima in 1535. It now is the sixth largest city in South America covering more than a thousand square miles and still growing. Pizarro considered it his greatest achievement. However, Pizarro had only six years in which to bask in the glory before he was assassinated; live by the sword, die by the sword.

His death permitted a slow, underground revival of the indigenous language of the Incas. Quechua had been banned in the late eighteenth century after the Spanish conquest. But it lived on, its survival aided by its extensive use between the indigenous peoples and the Spanish invaders.

There isn't much written material, which is a major obstacle to the teaching of Quechua, but it now shares official language status with Spanish in Peru.

The Martins have become proficient in Spanish, and its universal acceptance overcomes language hurdles, even when they visit the remote mountain regions of the country. They visited Machu Picchu once several years ago and climbed its steep terraces in awe. The focus of the trip seven hundred miles south of Lima had been to visit mission outposts in the hinterland, the area from which many of the poor have migrated to Lima.

An extract from an email recounts one of the early trips:

"Cheryl and I often shake our heads at God's amazing blessings ... This morning we went to the hospital for the poor at nine a.m. We gave them medical supplies. We expect blessings but when the Sisters here tell us they were a bit worried last night where more money was going to come from for supplies and we suddenly appear with $750, given to us by the Church of the Assumption [in Canada], it is so amazing to them and to us. Then we take out the supplies, they are telling us that these are the very things they needed. Amazing! Also, while we are handing out these medical supplies, our friend in Kingston was filling our van with more supplies from the Kingston General Hospital."

They met a Spanish surgeon working at the hospital, helped feed patients, and received an invitation to visit another area where the Sisters worked, "And it was only eleven thirty a.m."

Sister Dominga — "a great woman of God" (who apparently headed an orphanage) was from the Philippines. The Martins gave her money for the two homes she operated, which provided shelter and food for thirty-eight girls and twenty-eight boys.

The reach of the Catholic Church that Pizarro brought with him to Peru has flourished, even though it was introduced by the hated conquistador. More than 80 percent of the population described themselves as Catholics in 2014.

Pizarro's reign was followed by periodic uprisings, rebellions, and conquests over the years, with the most recent being between 1980 and 2000, when a terrorist organization called The Shining Path conducted a reign of terror. Nearly seventy thousand people were killed in those decades. Isolated outbursts of violence have continued into the current century.

While Peru is frequently lumped with third world countries — underdeveloped with widespread poverty — it stands apart in the field of education. The national University of San Marcos was founded in 1551 by Spanish Emperor Carlos, the same ruler who had given Pizarro sweeping powers a few years earlier. Depending on what resource is consulted, it is the oldest university in the Americas or, at the least the oldest in South America.

Either way, it is a prestigious institution of twenty faculties with more than 30,000 students. Peru's only Nobel Prize winner is among its alumni. Despite its size, however, this public university is not the largest in the country; the private *Universidad Nacional Mayor de San Marcos* is bigger.

In all, there are seventy-eight universities in the nation, with 500,000 students, testament to the explosion of interest in post-secondary education sweeping South America this century. But the complexity of the education system and questionable standards of some primary and secondary schools, make getting into university expensive. These realities spawned a proliferation of technical schools, not all of which have accreditation from the Ministry of Education. A blog by Fulbright Fellowship holder, Sabrina Karim, judged that the admission process meant that most Peruvians are not qualified to attend institutions of higher learning (America's Quarterly October, 2011).

It is within this reality, where the poor face daunting financial roadblocks, that HCTH is striving to help young people get through the school systems and at least give them a legitimate shot at further education.

Encouraging and helping children pursue education is fertile ground, particularly in the slums and mountain regions. A quarter to a third of children aged six to fourteen work, often putting in long hours at mining or construction sites. A 2014 demographic report explained that many "poor children temporarily or permanently drop out of school to help support their families."

Tom's preoccupation with education is both the carrot and the stick to the children they nurture.

What all this looks like depends on whose eyes are doing the looking. The Martins are unmoved by aggregated statistics or national trends. In the slums of Manchay, they ignore the numbers and concentrate on one child at a time. Does the child have enough to eat? Clothes to wear? A chance to go to school?

Through the wide-angled lens of the World Bank, its 2015 Peruvian overview states "The effects of strong growth on employment and income have significantly reduced poverty rates and boosted shared prosperity." Peru's vibrant fishing industry has Japan as a key market and, in some areas, potato production is an economic mainstay.

Between 2005 and 2013, poverty rates have more than halved, from about 45 percent of the population to 24 percent. It goes on to say that "there has been a dramatic decline of about 10 percentage points, from 16.4 percent to 6 percent of the population living below the official extreme poverty line."

Tell that to a father who rides a bus four hours a day in a fifteen-hour work day to scratch out a living for his family as a gardener, or to a fifteen-year-old mother subsisting with her infant in a hovel of cardboard and discarded wood. For that matter, tell it to the Martins, who see the underbelly of the national statistics.

Chapter 12
Lima

"EVERY DIRECTION LEADS TO TEEMING SLUMS."

The morning dew is a precious commodity in Lima, the second largest desert city in the world behind Cairo. Large nets on permanent structures along a section of the coast trap droplets to augment the inch or so of rain that falls each year on this city of 9 to 10 million. Clearly, it is not enough. The Rimac River, flowing down from the Andes, and wells are the principal water sources, but during the long, dry summers even these resources can be precarious.

Many parts of the slums around the city do not have a reliable source of water, and, by extension, few of the sanitary facilities taken for granted in North America. Those parts of the city are massive — some researchers reported that Lima had 30 percent of Peru's population in 1990, of which 70 percent lived in slums. There's little to suggest that those ratios have dramatically improved.

Water, or more precisely the lack of water, is a drag on the ability of the slum dwellers in Africa, Asia, and Latin America to loosen the chains of poverty. A WaterAid report prepared for World Water Day in 1996 said that slum dwellers spend

10-to-40 percent of their income on water purchased from private vendors, often at prices much higher than what public water systems charge. It is an observation that rings true. In Lima's slums, potable water is precious.

It is in one of those *barriadas*, a settlement or shantytown called Manchay, where the Martins are most active. There, more than fifty thousand people, mostly indigenous migrants drawn to the city from the highlands in search of a better future, scrape out an existence as poorly paid labourers or scrambling entrepreneurs doing odd jobs for pennies a day in an informal economy.

One better-off family with four children has a father who leaves before sunrise and returns after dark. He works as a gardener across the city, a two-hour or more commute each way, while his wife cleans houses in wealthier areas. Their house is made of wood, the floor is concrete, and there's a "water closet" indoors. A few hundred feet higher, almost directly above on the steep hillside, a neighbour has cages containing three or four ducks and a half dozen chickens outside a narrow two-room dwelling built of scavenged materials. Their outdoor privy is perched on another ledge higher up with access by an eight-foot ladder.

A new visitor wouldn't recognize the improvements made to individual dwellings, but the Martins take in the details; "See, they even have a fridge." Then there's the unexplainable: a Jacuzzi clinging to the edge of the hillside nowhere near water, running or otherwise.

While the land on which the city centre is built is basically flat, the city sprawl has climbed the hills in every direction, going ever higher with steeper slopes and worsening living conditions. Every direction from the city core leads to teeming slums.

And what constitutes a slum? Inadequate housing, in terms of materials; critical crowding levels, lack of services to remove excreta, a lack of good primary schools for children, and an insecure economic capacity. One researcher described them as communities — shantytowns — clinging precariously on the margins of society. In Manchay, the inhabitants also cling literally to the rock hillside that is their home.

We visited the Martins for a few days in Peru. What follows is a page of first impressions from my wife's diary:

November 1 Arrived about 8:30. Met by Cesar holding sign "Allen and Penny." Hand signals were the language. His car wheezed and bumped and the gears growled. He hunched over the wheel, jerking it back and forth as if he were an actor-driver in an old movie. Allen sat in back guarding our valuables which were on the floor under his feet. Cesar put them there, hidden from lurking thieves who apparently will break a window and grab stuff out of the hands of a passenger. It happened to one HCTH visitor, we were told.

Took more than an hour in steady, unpredictable, insane driving to get to La Molina where we are staying. The city looked black and dead. Could see even in the dark the outlines of grey empty mountains, which in the daylight are grey empty mountains except for people trying to survive on the bleak flanks.

We are staying in a comfortable hostel-like set-up [The Martins' Peruvian home]. Communal living room and kitchen which at the moment we are sharing with four kids from Southern California who are travelling through South America. Early twenties, no interest in American midterm elections yesterday. Our room is long, narrow with one small window high in the wall. Everything is fortified. High wall around the house but not high enough to keep Tom from climbing over it when he and Allen were locked out yesterday.

Dust covers everything, every day. A thick mantle falling from the stone mountains. It rains seldom. Just a grey mist at this time of year and an occasional mizzle at other times.

It is spring. Flowers are bright and cheerful in our gated community. Geraniums are small shrubs, perennial. Roses are so bright they glare in photos. In Manchay, there are a few flowers, some carefully tended, some wild and scraggly and dusty — like the whole place. But that comes later.

November 2, Sunday. Large church [with an] American pastor who has been here thirty years. November is mission month. Two sermons from two missionaries. One sidled up to asking outright for donations. The other was very slick. The sound system and translator — best I have ever heard anywhere.

In the afternoon we visited Manchay for the first time. Many homes, many families, many beautiful children and not beautiful parents, especially the women. They probably started out beautiful but their beauty has been ground out of them by poverty.

It was Miriam's twentieth birthday — a surprise party for her. She didn't know about the party or us. Although I think she knew about both. There was an outpouring of gratitude from her parents and her.

Monday, went by bus to grocery stores. We went to the market today [which is] next to a big shop. Market is smallish with wonderful fruits and vegetables, very fresh fish and meat. Chickens hanging cut open with innards showing eggs forming. Everything was very cheap and very good.

Unfortunately, the entries stopped, as the diary took a back seat for the rest of the week with the Martins — too much to see, too many people to visit, too many buses to ride.

We also missed a water main break that occurred a few days after our departure which flooded the Martin apartment. Tom reported that the floor was very clean, but the packed bags of clothes for distribution were very wet.

They live in a gated community, called Sol de la Molina, with a mixture of foreigners and better-off Peruvians. It is about a thirty minute bus ride from Manchay, the target area for the Martins' interventions, one of the newer *barriadas*, called *pueblos jo'venes*, in Lima. Settlement there began about twenty-five years ago, drawing many of the residents out of the mountain regions in search of employment.

Tom told of a Peruvian woman who lived in a prosperous part of Lima — and there are lots of them, too — who was riding the bus with friends into Manchay one day. As she gazed over the hillsides with their mishmash of shanties, her eyes filled with tears. She apparently said, "I didn't know people lived like that." And she didn't even get up close.

On the desert mountainside, pretty much the only thing that grows is the population. Clutches of hovels, some barely more substantial than tents, hide a multitude of couples and single mothers with flocks of kids at their feet. Still other dwellings house grandmothers who might have a half dozen small children to care for. The luckier people have a metal roof over their heads.

Trucks wend their way up the narrow roads, their progress marked by billowing clouds of dust. (Locals bring up bricks by wheelbarrows.) Some of the trucks carry water — and as the terrain gets tougher, the cost of water goes up. Those trucks, with their water cargo of questionable quality, come by most days in the valley, but the hillside climb to replenish jerry cans and jugs is less certain and depends entirely on the disposition of the vendors.

The residents are among the two million plus Peruvians who don't have easy access to potable water. One news story reported that the hill-dwellers are paying up to six times as much for water than are their nearby and more affluent city neighbours.

Strings of laundry hang from all manner of lines or fences. Basins of water serve several functions, before the dregs may be used to water a lonely geranium blooming bravely in the parched earth beside a dwelling of wood, tin, and cardboard.

Glass windows are so rare that they attract attention; a youngster would like to look through one.

The conventional shantytowns — *barriadas convencionales* — have no planned layouts or roads, nor land reserves for public services. They occupy marginal lands and are home to about 20 percent of the shantytown population. Many residents are squatters. Then, there are *barriadas asistidas* — "assisted shantytowns." During a period of rapid growth, land ownership in the desert zone was assigned to the state in 1961; these lands featured a plan for residences, roads and public services. About 60 percent of the shantytown population live in these assisted communities.

The process of obtaining title to land in these assisted communities can be as torturous as it is vital. A water pipe can be tantalizingly close, but a resident is barred from tying into it without a land title document. Luckily, since the average age of the population is lower than in the city as a whole, these dwellers have more time to wade through the bureaucratic jungle. Also fortunately, they are determined, resilient and patient.

One observer noted that "people in Lima's squatter settlements rely on their wits to overcome any obstacles thrown up by government."

Peruvians, by nature, are also an industrial and optimistic people, so, while to the outsider, the situation in places like Manchay looks bleak, the oft-repeated phrase is that things are getting better. Even the Martins see great progress, with concrete steps going part way up the hillside in several areas before giving way to narrow, rocky paths. In newer parts of the province, there are some paved roads, electricity, and water. However, such improvements are often incomplete; poverty still persists, and much of the population continues to be ignored.

It is striking that *barriadas* residents don't look at themselves as being poor, and their generosity is noteworthy, reflecting a trait that we observed everywhere in Peru. One of the rare panhandlers on the bus, with her bandaged arm over what was alleged to be a burn, had passengers searching their pockets for a coin, even though the scam was obvious. The approach was gentle, just an outreached hand. The interaction drew attention, because begging seems such a rarity. A blind musician may play his violin, or an elderly person may sell penny candy. They are offering something, which makes the begging more palatable.

Visitors to the tourist town of Cusco, relatively close to Machu Picchu, do encounter women in traditional gowns and hats, often with similarly attired babies on their hips, wanting to pose for pictures in exchange for a coin or two. They are too proud, however, to linger or accost a visitor.

Peruvian guide books tell visitors to be aware of the culture of exchange that, should you give something to a local, the recipient will find something in his or her possession to give in return. We were invited to meals often in Manchay despite the fact that the families had barely enough food for themselves; small gifts are pressed on visitors — a proud and lovely custom that underlines the two-way street of giving and receiving.

Chapter 13
Charity Auction

"ONE MORE STORY..."

— Tom Martin

It was the last Saturday of October in Napanee, a week before Halloween, and a few days before the Martins were leaving for Peru. A steady stream of cars turned off Centre Street, just past Canadian Tire, Wal-Mart, and a Dollar Store. But those icons of Canadian life weren't the destination. It was the Strathcona Paper Centre, the arena which, as in countless Canadian communities, is as much a locus for community as a shopping mall.

Its parking lot was filling up with cars unloading two distinct streams of people. One group shepherded herds of kids dragging hockey bags to the main entrance, and the second, generally an older bunch, walked with purpose toward an unmarked door held open by a smiling senior.

A dozen volunteers at a row of tables welcomed arrivals: the first two collected five dollars a person, the next four offered bidding paddles. Behind them, just like the noisy migrating crows outside, were about two hundred gossiping, shopping, laughing, noisy guests at the Helping Cope Through Hope annual charity auction.

Visitors were registered and then funnelled past perimeter tables loaded with items for the silent auction. The purpose of the groupings — numbers one to fifty, fifty-one to one-hundred, and so on — would become apparent as the night wore on. There were classy flashlights, knitted tams and scarves, artwork from Africa and Peru, golf balls, a food steamer, a portable baby bed — 250 items in all, donated by individuals and companies, as well as suitcases of country-specific crafts brought to Canada by the Martins.

Soon, the instructions came. The closing time for the tables during the silent auction would be in thirty-minute intervals, implicitly allowing bidders to move up a table for a similar item should they be outbid on the first-of-a-kind. A brigade of about twenty, mostly teenagers wearing T-shirts identifying HCTH, hovered nearby.

Tom, noticing a lost-looking yellow-shirted youngster, placed an arm around his shoulder and pointed out an assignment to the eager, nodding student.

There was good-natured elbowing as bidders sought to beat the competition, stretching to see if their bid had been surpassed. It was fun and lucrative, a win-win where buyers collected inexpensive treasures and the dollars mounted up for the Martins. Only very large items had a reserve bid, although some things, such as a small exquisitely carved elephant, sparked a real bidding war. Eventually, it sold at forty-five dollars, still a bargain.

Many of the articles, particularly carvings, had been purchased in Uganda or Zambia by the Martins specifically for this event. The bidders for the forty-five dollar elephant had already cased out the location of other elephants on tables not yet closed.

"Five minutes before bidding closes on items one to fifty. One of our helpers will label each winning item for you to see what you bought," says Tom and continues in the same breath. "You'll see a photograph at the back wall. That's Annet. And the other picture is Annet with her friend Barbara, and the girl in the yellow dress is her daughter Kate. This is an amazing story." It was also a familiar one to anyone following the Martins in their summer of visits to North American churches and community organizations.

Who these women are and where they fit into the Martin universe has much more depth but, for this event where the audience consists mostly of HCTH supporters, just the mention is sufficient.

Barbara, who had been a beneficiary of Helping Cope Through Hope, had appealed to the Martins on behalf of her friend, Annet. Her daughter, little Kate, had dropped out of school because Annet couldn't pay the fees. The Martins protested that most of their funds had already been distributed. They were down to their last few dollars. Tom pauses and clears his throat. "I get a little choked up when I talk about some of these kids. What would happen to little Kate? What are you going to do?"

He wondered how they could go home and leave Annet abandoned. They didn't, and he continued the story.

Annet had been skin and bones, flirting with death that January. By mid-summer, she had changed into a robust, smiling young woman. Healthy food, and medical care made the difference and were paid for with HCTH dollars. In fact, her transformation was so great that Tom didn't recognize her the following year. Her sponsor, listening to the story he helped write, flatly declared it a miracle.

Tom added a footnote: "I took her, Barbara, and three others to a football game [where another sponsored child was playing], and Annet was jumping, cheering, and shouting along with the rest of them."

The auction closed on one table and the momentary hush gave way to the scrambling to see who bought what and, for the losers, what could be had on the next table.

Some attendees came from communities as far as 250 kilometres away, but the majority were locals, including a large contingent from the Roblin Wesleyan church, as well as friends and family from the internet circle.

The announcement: "The bidding on table four will end in five minutes" signals another "Amazing story…"

The education of many orphan children the Martins met was thwarted because they had no reliable homes. So, even if HCTH were to pay their school fees, their poor living arrangements often made the education hill too high to climb. Other kids, whose homes were far into the countryside, faced a similar obstacle.

It was a reality that weighed heavily on them, and Tom told a new friend about how the Martins wished for a home for some of these Ugandan children. The man listened as Tom painted a picture of their bleak future.

After a brief silence, the man asked, "How much would it cost to buy a house?"

Just a casual conversation, it seemed, but for Tom, the idea of an HCTH-owned home for students had already taken shape. He said he had been casually house shopping, an activity that stokes possibly even more interest in Uganda than in Canada. Word-of-mouth is the dominant way for bringing buyers and sellers together, and "everyone wants to help." It is exciting business in a land of not much excitement. He had found a four-bedroom house in good nick for $20,000.

"I'll buy it," said the Canadian, and then, after digesting that decision, wondered aloud what the cost would be for having someone stay with the children and look after them for a year. Whatever the cost, the donor would take it on. Details about the donor, the house and his commitment are described in more detail later.

"That was two weeks ago," Tom told the bidders, then switched gears again. "Time is up; bidding is closed. We'll be having the live auction right after the last table sale is finished. You'll be able to buy all this." He gestured around the platform at goods ranging from fresh garlic to hand-made quilts, bushels of apples and preserves. He paid special attention to the dozen or more pies baked by Cheryl. "I peeled the apples," he boasted, but allowed that several close friends had also pitched in.

Fifteen minutes later, as the auctioneer moved into place, Tom said, "One more story." It was the story of Joan and a man who said he'd like to send two young people to university. He was not daunted by the cost: $1,800 a year for three years. Each. "Sure," he said, and Joan became his ward.

So he was intrigued when Tom told supporters a few days later that Joan's father was in danger of losing the family home because of an unpaid debt at the bank, money borrowed to help an older sister attend school.

"The man asked if this was the same Joan that he was sending to university, and I said yes. He asked how much he owed, and I said $1,200. And he said the cheque was in the mail."

A murmur ran through the crowd but Tom, the ultimate story teller, wasn't finished yet. The man had enquired about sending two students to university. Joan was one. Did the offer for a second student still hold? It did.

So then there was Floribert, a twenty-five-year-old man who had graduated from secondary school about four years ago and wanted to go to university, but was financially incapable. Now he was going.

Tom started to wind down, but not before telling the folks about a student acquaintance who survived on one meal a day, costing about sixty-five cents, which was all he could afford while going to university.

The auctioneer was ready to go, and, likely unnecessarily, Tom encouraged the crowd to give generously, as all money went directly to the mission field.

In an aside to a companion, one spectator praised the whole event as highly organized and professional. It was an interesting observation about an organization that strives hard to maintain its down-home, "aw-shucks" persona; an organization Tom said he didn't want to grow so big that they could no longer oversee every element.

"The tenth annual charity auction is over," he said. "God blessed this fundraiser again. People were so good to give items to sell, to help at the auction, and to attend the auction and buy items. We raised $10,811. [The figure rose to just under $12,000 when subsequent contributions were added.] I hope each of you is saying 'WOW!' God is good. This money will do so much in Peru, Zambia, and Uganda. This is the first time we have been over $10,000."

Chapter 14
Among the Martins' Followers

"PREACH THE GOSPEL AT ALL TIMES AND,
WHEN NECESSARY, USE WORDS."

— Francis of Assisi

The mission odyssey of the Martins began with the children of Peru.
They gathered them up on the street corners of the slums, the
edges of the schoolyards, or through a suggestion from another
missionary. Tom and Cheryl learned their names, met their
families — if they had families — and won their trust.

They were kids like Milagros, whose name means Miracle, a
four-year-old who would jump into Tom's arms each time they
visited her home. Milagros' mother had suffered from acute
arthritis and the Martins came by often, bringing medication for
the mother and providing food for her and her children. There
were also gifts for Milagros — teddy bears, clothes, and a little
pair of rubber boots. Even when the mother's health improved
sufficiently that she could support the family, the bond with
Milagros held firm.

A few years later, in Canada, Tom and Cheryl's ten-year-old
granddaughter, Maddie, had received ten dollars as a gift. She

gave it to her grandparents to be used to help a child in their mission. Tom reported on what the gift provided.

"A highlight today was taking Milagros to the market to buy some items she needed.

We thought Milagros was a good choice because she is the same age as Maddie. We bought her three pairs of socks, six pairs of underwear, bananas (her favourite fruit) and ten buns. She was very happy." Tom was, too.

The kind of connections with Milagros' family is a familiar refrain running through emails which describe the help provided by the Martins to families beset by financial and/ or medical problems. Food is key. One email said they visited homes of four families, bringing food for two people they considered were most desperate — a dozen tangerines, fourteen buns, butter, canned milk, and cooking oil for each. Then they stopped in at another home where the mother of four young children had been killed in a car accident a few days before. The husband was unwell. They left food there as well.

"We told them it was a gift from God. We asked them if they went to church. They said they went to the Roman Catholic Church. We said that we serve the same God and we wanted to bless them."

Meeting the physical needs was the first imperative, getting the kids into school was the next one.

It was stories such as these, along with our curiosity about how HCTH worked on the ground, that caused my wife and me to "follow the Martins" to Peru. We knew we would meet Miriam, one of the children we had been sponsoring at arm's length. Names scattered haphazardly through successive emails would become real people. As our travel date grew closer, our anticipation rose in the furious flurry of emails between us and the Martins.

Tom and Cheryl had arrived in Peru three days before us, late in 2014. Tom said that he had only three hours sleep after a middle-of-the-night arrival — "there was too much on my mind." He and Cheryl raced through the household chores of unpacking and sorting the mounds of clothing they brought to give away.

They hooked up with Karina, their on-the-ground representative, who lives close by. Together, along with her husband Javier, they made the circuit to the Moli Centro, a commercial area, to change money at a better exchange rate than they could in Canada, and then to buy groceries, fruits and vegetables.

We would soon learn, first-hand, that Tom's energy was unflagging, and that his mind flies in six directions at once, a characteristic evident in his broadcast email at the end of that first day:

"It is nice to be back in Peru again. A perfect example of how God works things out happened today. I mentioned to Javier that the sponsors of a boy gave us money to buy four chickens. It just so happened that another family had given money for that family, so I gave the money to Javier to build a cage for the chickens. Javier can build a metal cage because Mark, who came from Canada last year, taught him how to forge steel and bought him the tools he needs … Cheryl just peeled a mango. We say that the best mangos in the world are in Peru."

The next sentence talks about the temperature and that their plane, with their luggage, had arrived five minutes early.

Our first full day in Peru followed a "schedule" that Tom had in mind, though no one else really knew the components. Cheryl explained that he did the planning, she did the following. We all knew the highlights, and the details would unfold: we'd go to church, exchange North American currency for Peruvian soles (exchange rate, depending on the day, was 2.5 – 3 soles to a US$1), catch a bus to Manchay, and visit some folks, including Miriam.

We started with a brisk walk — the only kind there is when following Tom — through the gated community, to a modern church building where many ex-pats and missionaries worship. The pastor is an aging American who has been in Peru for years, but this day was the beginning of a month on mission emphasis, so he was mainly master of ceremonies to introduce guest speakers.

The congregation had a goal of raising $43,000, some of which would be earmarked for an orphanage for HIV-infected children in an African city. The fund-raising challenge was a leap of faith for the congregation; it is not wealthy. At the appointed start time, there were only a handful of people in the sanctuary. Others slowly drifted in during the first half of the service, which prompted a whispered explanation that people "aren't very prompt here." When the preaching started, about 150 people filled the pews.

The first of two speakers was from a jungle mission who asked for support in reaching out to remote settlements and for prayer for his wife who has "pain for her age; she can't jump rope, my girl." Arthritis. The second, a glib son of a minister, preached a gospel "that changes, transforms lives." Offering plates moved quietly along the pews like a well-oiled machine.

A visitor might have wondered about the emphasis on "spreading the gospel" in other places, while we were in Lima to see a mission project in action. It is commonplace, however. This church had a project in Germany; a Bahamian congregation we know sends a team to Canada. Others had their sights on the United States.

One explanation for the outreach numbers is in the numbers. Reporter Jessica Martinez wrote in the *Christian Post*, July 19, 2013, that it was predicted that there would be 2.6 billion Christians world-wide by 2020, with most of the growth coming in the global south, while Christianity will decline in the global north from 91 percent in 1970 to 76.9 percent in 2020. Much of that decline would be in Canada, where the Christian population fell from 94.5 percent of the population in 1970, to 69.4 percent in 2010, and is expected to drop to 66 percent by 2020.

With the missionary messages still ringing in our ears, we headed to Manchay aboard a public transit system bus, at first an unsettling experience. We quickly learned that the drivers actually knew what they were doing, and were doing it very well. Strangely, the chaotic system works more or less efficiently on Lima's main streets — three, four, maybe five vehicles drive abreast in a constant game of chicken. Hesitate, and two vehicles have squeezed in front. Lean on the horn, maybe close your eyes, and go. That bus? Two inches away? Go, go, go. One of two things happens: either a hole opens, or you slam to a stop. We never experienced the third option. Nor did we even see any accidents, not even minor fender-benders.

Buses bump and lurch, a roller-coaster ride for a fare of one sole from Molina to Manchay. Even when packed to overflowing, a head of white hair, or no hair, or an infant in tow will get you a seat. Sunday buses, however, are less crowded, so Tom has a moment to strike up a conversation with a youngster and his mother. Soon there's laughter and a Spanish "God bless" as they part.

Outside the window, the slipping standard of living, as evidenced by roadside structures, is not well-defined, but reveals itself silently, block by block. A large church, perhaps Catholic, for this is a Catholic nation, relieves the monotony of cheek-to-jowl store fronts or maybe residences (Stores are the ones with the door open). Farther along is a public school, large and substantial, dominating the landscape. Prominent among the haphazard structures around the school's edges is a well-maintained basketball court, a common feature in public spaces.

In the heart of Manchay — at least we think it is the heart — street merchants are at work, selling produce or prepared food from push carts. Little children and dogs dart in and out around and through the legs of merchants and shoppers alike. A litre of freshly picked strawberries costs a sole, maybe less — if one chooses to barter over a penny.

Following the double-time march of Tom, we wove around pedestrians and scruffy dogs along roadways covered in dust that permeates everything. It's a desert, after all, where every wind storm rearranges the terrain.

Tom knocked on a door, peered through a small porthole, and called a name. The door slowly opened, a burst of excited greetings, hugs and, for the kids, suckers. Introductions. This wasn't our destination, so the stop was brief.

Our first "official" stop was Anna's place, a door in the middle of what, in Canada, would pass for a tired one-car garage. Tom rapped on the door, then opened it. "Anna?" No answer. "Guess she's not home. We'll have to come back." Anna . is a teenager once helped with school fees, and now a single mother and a drop-out. She gets food stuffs from Helping Cope Through Hope.

Names blend and stories merge as we walk along but some underlying themes are relentless. Teenage pregnancy seems to be a rite of passage into the abyss of poverty for young girls in Grade Eleven, fathers gone — but back just often enough to add to the growing brood left behind without adequate clothing, food, or medical care. There was resignation in the voices of the Martins as they recounted yet another example.

A Canadian woman sponsored a girl, travelled to Peru several times and developed a close personal attachment. Outings together, shopping for school supplies. The sponsor had visions of a promising future for this youngster. She would graduate from high school and college and escape the ghetto into a better life. Pregnancy shattered that dream.

"No, the donor isn't bitter, just deeply disappointed. She had such high hopes," said Tom, who explained that the support level from the Canadian sponsor has changed, and the relationship irreparably altered.

As we walked, sidewalks gave way to paths, ever narrowing as they wind up and up the barren, grey hillside plastered with makeshift shelters. Tom veered off, pointed several hundred feet upward. "See those orange pants? That's where we're going." Those trousers, in the distance, were flapping in the wind off the corner of a dwelling high above us.

"There's been a lot of improvements here in the last ten years," he said as we climbed the dirt hillside with rarely a rock to give purchase. Cheryl and Penny fell behind as Tom leapt ahead. The climb was punctuated with catch-your-breath breaks which enabled us to survey the dwellings chipped into the rock face. And the squalor.

A small child, perhaps two, crawled along the path in front of his home. The path, thirty inches wide, hugged the house along the edge of a sheer cliff face, dropping twenty or thirty feet. How do these babies know not to tumble over the edge? Even here there must be angels.

We stopped at a couple of dwellings. The introductions at each were similar. Tom knocked on a door, waited for a minute, pushed it open, and called a name. Sometimes an occupant would appear, enthusiastic greetings would get exchanged and we were introduced in Spanish. Responses were in smiles, gestures, and the traditional Peruvian welcome of a hug and an air-kiss.

"Come back here," beckoned Tom from the side of one dwelling. "Last year we [Tom and Dan] chipped out the rock here so that they can add a room." It looked like solid rock, but apparently sledge hammers had done the trick. Up about eight feet were two tiny cages, one housing chickens, and the other guinea pigs.

While the Martins buy chicks, rabbits and guinea pigs for families, the criteria for selecting recipients are unclear. Everyone hopes the livestock will propagate but, ultimately, they end up in a pot. One young boy, asked what happened to the guinea pig given to him last year, smiled and rubbed his stomach. "Yum yum."

Visits are short and Tom said there were many homes on his list. In one, a young boy got a couple of tee-shirts and a pair of shorts. In another, a girl didn't get her gift of clothing because the Martins had misjudged her size. It would arrive on a subsequent visit.

In the Martins' apartment, rented from Kids Alive, one of the four bedrooms has two sets of bunk beds. The lower ones are reserved for visiting supporters, and the uppers are transformed into a carefully sorted clothing depot. Each day before they begin their trek, the Martins identify individuals they will likely encounter, and clothing gifts are stuffed into backpacks for them.

Descending, we arrived at a somewhat more substantial home. The door swung open accompanied by a babble of greetings, and we were invited in. It was a thinly disguised surprise — Tom loves surprises — because Miriam lived here with her family, and today was her birthday. For us the surprise was to visit on her birthday, for her the surprise was that her sponsors would be there to celebrate with her. In reality, it was a surprise for no one, but that didn't dampen the festivities in any way.

Birthdays in Peru are a really big deal. Sixteen people had gathered for the party, and, mostly in sign language punctuated with gales of laughter, worked hard to make us welcome. Two young women provoked a moment of panic for us when they entered the room: we weren't sure which one was Miriam. Then she smiled, her whole body smiled, and we knew. The other girl was Sylvia, a cousin "from the mountains" who lived with the family while she attended school. She hung back.

Miriam came to us with outstretched arms, and I was rocked by an unexpected wave of emotion. This was the little girl we'd been supporting at arm's length, who annually sent us letters (often left unanswered because I was uncomfortable about getting close), who was now this lovely young woman. How do you explain your irrational distance from someone who, with a couple of English words, asks in anticipation if you read her letters and cracks your heart open in that moment?

Peruvians are huggers and air-kissers. Both cheeks, every time you meet. After greeting Miriam, we hugged her parents, a sister, a brother, a cousin, an aunt, and a handful of neighbours. Everyone, from the oldest to the youngest. We said truthfully, for-goodness-knows-how-many times, that we very much liked Peru. And, had they asked, we could have been equally truthful in admitting their welcome and openness were almost overwhelming.

Miriam was delighted to be the centre of attention on "her day," and said so in a speech that we mostly didn't understand. It was about thanking God for us — "her angels" —, the Martins, and God for divine interventions during earlier family illnesses.

Then, it was time to sing — "Do you sing?"

"No"

"Do you dance?"

"Not for forty years." (The questions were mostly deductions.)

Tom disappeared, leaving Cheryl as the sole translator, but she couldn't carry the load single-handedly. Gestures, plus a stew of unrelated English and Spanish words, kept the conversation going in fits and starts. Miriam and her mother also disappeared, only to reappear shortly with bowls of fruit, fresh from the jungle, followed by an offer of paper towels to wipe up the drips of the sweet juice.

Tom burst through the door, bearing a huge birthday cake with enough calories in the icing to give a dietitian heart failure. Holding and munching through the giant pieces of cake broke through any residue of reserve. How can you look dignified with icing on your nose? The paper towels were pressed into service again.

Then, Miriam brought out her assignment books for her second year of physiotherapy and speech therapy. The quality of her writing and illustrations said even to a foreigner that this girl was an extraordinary student, dedicated to forging a future that would break the chains of Manchay. Our chests swelled with pride.

The laughter and chatter had subsided, and we were watching the Martins for a departure signal, when little Kelly, who had been hovering around my wife's chair all evening, made her move. Or was it Penny who made the move? Anyway, that was how we acquired our next Peruvian charge. When she gets a bit older, I suppose it will be okay if she calls us parents.

With the party over, it was time for hugs again. Genuine hugs, this time. Poor Sylvia hung back — it wasn't her party.

There are a handful of back stories there. First, there's Karina, a thirty-something bubbly woman on-the-ground administrator. The Martins met her when they first went to Peru with Kids Alive. She was a young woman from the mountains who had studied accounting. Each month, she ensures that money sent by HCTH supporters reaches the designated individuals and is spent for its designated purposes. She's also the Martins' eyes and ears. When a student misses classes, she's the one that raises the red flag with the Martins and proposes remedial action.

Karina's husband, Javier, is a Columbian who had spent a year in the mountains, ministering and living among the natives. Like most people in the region, he's short, stocky, swarthy, and attentive. It was easy to see why the Martins were attracted to this couple who, now, "are almost like our own missionaries."

For our part, our conversations with them were limited to gestures, nods and smiles as we worked around the language barrier. An odd word in French was close enough to a Spanish equivalent for a eureka moment, or when Karina's rudimentary English and electronic translation device — given to her by a visiting Canadian — collided with a phrase that we all understood.

Karina and Javier acted as our tour guides for one happy day of learning, communicating, and laughing, wandering around the oldest parts of the city. Our lunch was a traditional Peruvian dish that we were enjoying when we learned that Javier, while in the jungle, dined on snakes with the locals. Did you really? Big grin and nod. Then, gesturing, he showed how one would hold the snake, bite off the head, spit it out, and eat the rest. Whether he was leading us on or not wasn't clear... but we passed on dessert.

Karina and Javier's home near the Martins is along a walkway adorned with flowers and ornaments that reflect the interests of the residents. Walk through their front door, across the sparkling main floor, and up the stairs to a second level, and you find a flat roof resembling a construction site: a pile of sand, bricks, some iron bars, and briquettes scattered around a horseshoe-shaped structure under a partial, corrugated-steel roof. Javier proudly presented his rooftop blacksmith shop.

He pointed to a forge that Mark from Canada created with materials available in Peru to teach Javier the basics of blacksmithing. Mark is a retired craftsman who had been the resident blacksmith in a museum, where his job was demonstrating the skills that were vital to Canadian pioneers of an earlier era.

In its early days, Javier's forge attracted the attention of the fire department, which had a dim view of the rooftop venture. The issue was resolved with the construction of a partial concrete enclosure which hid the glow of red-hot coals and sparks. A chicken coop was just one of his projects: it would make its home on the edge of a steep embankment as a home for four chickens already pecking out their existence. Now the chicken population could double. He was also fashioning window frames for a local church building.

The owners of those chickens were one of about ten families we visited one day as the Martins darted from one hillside shanty to another.

On these and subsequent visits over the week, Tom sometimes quietly disappeared to resurface a short time later with a bag of foodstuffs from a neighbourhood vendor, which might include a bottle of soda pop if the visit was likely to be extended. The host would magically produce a bowl of a local, popular fruit, somewhat like a pomegranate, that grows wild in the mountain jungle.

Depending on the circumstances, arrangements were often made for a visit to a household to deliver foodstuffs from the supermarket or clothes and supplies for a child. Or, particularly with teenagers sponsored for school, plans were hatched to take them out for dinner as a special treat. One of Tom's emails reported, "We ate in Manchay at a restaurant called *lo de Juan*. Instead of salad, we got extra chips with the chicken. We needed Mark to help us clean up the chips. It did work out, as we took a lot to our friend Alejandro, his wife and three little girls." Nothing, not even the smallest thing, goes to waste in the Martin world.

The restaurant is one of the numerous chicken establishments in Manchay which, generally, serve fried chicken far superior to the quality of chicken restaurant chains in North America.

Helpings of chicken are huge and accompanied with fresh French fries, always enough for the guests to take a bag of leftovers home to share with family members. That, in itself, is special, because many young people have never been to a restaurant before. The leftovers enable them to share their experience of restaurant fare while describing the checkered tablecloths, heaping baskets, and jugs of Chicha, a non-alcoholic beverage known here as "beer."

A highlight from another day that week was a visit to a new family in the steadily expanding spider web of connections, high on the hills. The mother in the first home became a Christian recently, Tom said, and was enthusiastic about the transformation this event brought to her life. Her husband was spending more time at home, rather than out with his friends. The Martins delivered some clothes to her, and were also taking clothes to the women's sister who had had twins twenty-one months ago. The sister's husband had abandoned her before the children were born.

The Martins' descriptions always are cryptic, leaving the listener to imagine the surroundings and what the individuals look like. Are they old? Young? The focus is totally on giving aid, providing hope — at least that part is explicit.

How else could one describe their visit a few years back to Yurimaguas, a thriving port-town — says Wikipedia — or a sleepy town, says Lonely Planet — of more than 60,000. It sits in the steamy rainforest at the confluence of two mighty rivers that flow into the Amazon. From its rarely used airport, the Martins travelled for nearly four hours on 122 kilometres of roads so slippery even Tom's emails were bug-eyed.

Tom Martin has always downplayed the many adventures, and misadventures that spice up their travels off the beaten track. I knew they had had those kinds of events when we joined them in Peru. Our own tourist experience, however, reinforced the reality that the unexpected is the expected, and that danger is a constant companion. In a letter home, Penny described an outing from the lodge deep in the jungle where we stayed for a few days, and is included here as an example of such unexpected dangers.

We flew from Lima to Puerto Maldonado on the banks of the Madre de Dois River which flows into the Amazon — 46 degrees Celsius when we landed. Went up river in a dugout type boat with a canopy, a motor and life jackets — note the presence of same. [I had picked up a bug, leaving her on her own the following days to do the excursions, including a cruise on a lagoon in a small dugout canoe into a large lake described as calm and placid.]

Walked about four kilometres on a jungle track, mostly a stream bed. Tarantulas live here. Arrived at the lagoon [which] could have been a scene from the Heart of Darkness: skies darkening, water still and black, trees hanging low over it. The lagoon is a passage through a deep swamp — no dry land at all. Anacondas live here.

Loaded into a boat which had seats for eight. No canopy, no life jackets, no bailers, no motor. Setting the scene here. We came out onto the lake which was calm enough to see a caiman eying our boat. We eyed it back. The storm hit suddenly, great cracks of thunder and lightning and a wind tearing across the lake. Boat rapidly filled with water and I knew we were in trouble when the guide picked up a sponge about the size of his hand to mop it up. The boatman had a knife which the guide used to cut all our water bottles in half to use as bailers. So, a few bailers, the boatman steering, or trying to and two paddlers — the guide and me.

Obviously we survived, but we were in real danger of swamping. By the time we made it back into the lagoon, the gunnels were only three inches above water. We figured that if Allen had been with us, we'd have sunk since the boat would have been at full capacity. [Divine providence in the shape of a bug that laid me flat for twenty-four hours? Tom would say it was a God thing.] Another group was huddled under a small shelter. One of them told me later they didn't think we were going to make it — so low in the water — but it turned out they were in as much danger as we were because a tree was struck by lightning about fifteen feet

from where they were huddled. Did I mention that in the lake,
aside from the caimans, there were four species of piranhas?
     So we emptied our rubber boots and walked back through the
muddy river that the track had become.

The Martins' experience of crossing streams on "the worst roads you have ever been on, times ten" seemed somewhat at odds with the descriptions offered tourists of the "paved road." Tom claimed it was even muddier and slippery than the previous year, but it was worth it to be able to visit and bring supplies to the home for malnourished babies.

The destination was a community that included a mission home the Martins had visited the previous year. Fifteen babies and children, mostly Chayweatans, were cared for by the missionaries, including a boy named Martin. The Martins had met Martin the previous year, when he had turned up unaccompanied and nursing a serious injury to his foot. He had travelled, he said, with his ten-year-old cousin, an explanation that left the missionaries scratching their heads — no one knew how they got there, since their home was a two-day boat ride away.

The Martins bought bags of rice, sugar (fifty kilograms each), and beans (twenty kilograms) for the children. The home operators reminded them that, the year before, they arrived with food donations when "the staff and wards of the mission had no food to eat." The Martins had also left cash to be used for purchasing medical supplies and for helping mothers return to their homes after giving birth.

They had also visited a mission-sponsored farm at Tarapoto, where boys were taught how to be farmers, how to produce garden crops, and raise livestock, to end the cycle of malnutrition. Without this type of intervention, the natives' food staple is a yucca or manioc root that is fermented. The predictable outcome is intoxication, even among the very young, including newborns who may come into the world addicted.

Without details, Tom reported that money that was left at both the missions was a good sum for the children's home, "thanks to a friend," and "money two couples gave us" for the farming operation.

Later, back in Lima, the Martins visited a home for girls to provide money to repair their two bathrooms, and then onto another home, for boys. The house mother here was someone the Martins had known since their first Peruvian assignments in 2003 whose daughter, Gaby, had been sponsored in 2006 by HCTH. They had attended a recital by Gaby, who is now a talented violinist whose mother had once scrimped to pay for music lessons.

After a full day of walking through dusty streets and climbing hills, Tom was looking forward to a shower — if the water was warm... and it wasn't. Then, Cheryl flushed the toilet and the shower turned warm, then cold again, until she flushed it again. Why? Who knows, but that ended the email.

Chapter 15
Donor Travel

"SHE TOOK A PIECE OF MY HEART."
— Jane Fournier

"Peru awaits you with open doors," said a letter from Miriam, the school girl we had sponsored for several years.

She was twenty as of 2014, on the threshold of completing her training as a physiotherapist, fulfilling a dream to become a professional and becoming "able to help my parents because, I love them a lot." She was expansive in expressing her appreciation— "I love you a lot. I want to say that I am very happy to have parents like you."

Calling us parents jolted me. When we went to Peru, we didn't know all fear of "getting too close" would vanish when this shy, young woman with the charcoal eyes and a million-dollar smile greeted us.

Sure, she said in her letters that she wanted to greet us with "a strong hug and kiss," but this was the real thing. We stood, silently for a moment, letting the emotions flow over us as her family and relatives looked on.

Tom had told us earlier how their bond with Miriam's family came about. They had learned that her mother was seriously ill and had begun visiting the home to offer help.

Her mother asked the Martins why it was that they would come to visit her every other day. She said, "I am a Catholic, and the priest never comes to pray for me, but you come every two days to my house and pray."

Tom explained that church affiliation was not an issue for them, they simply wanted to help. He added that they were moved to help Miriam further her education when they saw the quality of her school work.

"I told her mother that we never pick children on the basis of where they go to church, or even if they go to church. We select children who appear to have potential, whether they are Protestant, Catholic, Muslim, or nothing. They are all people who we believe that God has led into our path."

Variations of the scene that day, when we met Miriam and her family, have been played out countless times for HCTH supporters who follow the Martins into one of the three countries in which they serve. Peru, given its many natural attractions including Machu Picchu, is the most popular.

What the supporters do during the visits is wide open, but most choose to become engaged in projects, or to work directly with students.

THE BEDFORDS

Dan and Nancy Bedford of Sunbury, Ontario, have been to Peru more than once, and have sponsored several children. Turns out, the Bedfords also had a hand in Miriam's educational support when, unknown to us, our annual contribution was insufficient to cover her educational expenses. The Bedford's donations covered the shortfall because, true to the Martins' commitment not to solicit money directly, the Martins hadn't said a word to us.

If no donations would cover it, the Martins would have personally made up the difference. Miriam's education would not go short.

Dan Bedford and Tom have been friends for nearly sixty years, a boyhood link made when their families were in the same rural community just north of Kingston, which might explain the type of projects undertaken by the "retired" school teacher and the accountant. For example, in 2013, when Dan went to Peru on his own for three weeks, he and Tom tackled a back-breaking project at Mari's clapboard and patched-together hillside home.

Mari could be the poster child for mission work in Manchay. Pregnant and desperate as a very young teenager, she foraged for food, pleaded with anyone and everyone for help, so that her baby "wouldn't have to live like this." She met stone walls every day, until a representative from Kids Alive heard her plea and brought her to the Oasis, the shelter/school Kids Alive operates.

Mari, with her magnetic personality and heart-warming transformation, is now one of the Oasis staff, and a favourite example of the Martins' eclectic approach to missions.

Dan and Tom cleared out and replaced a section of a veneer-like rear wall of Mari's home which had been damaged, leaving her house vulnerable to break-ins. While they were at it, they cleared and levelled another patch of the mountainside, breaking up the rock and shovelling out the rubble so that there would be room to add a bathroom. It would replace the outhouse ten steps up the mountain, which was not only inconvenient but unhealthy.

Mari had longed for a bathroom, but getting the legal title to her property seemed an insurmountable bureaucratic challenge, and, without it, she could not get running water. Dan, who had helped her buy the property, also untangled those knots. Now, working with Tom, the bathroom project was taking shape.

It's not clear which shovelful of dirt spawned Dan's idea of launching his "pay forward" project in Manchay. Dan explained to Tom that he still had a bit of money to spend in Manchay, and who knew better how to use the money than the people who live there. He thought a pay forward project would work among the girls he had met the previous year at a Bible Club. Tom agreed.

The response excited him. Four girls committed to making someone's life a little bit better. "I was amazed at how they reacted to the question of how they would feel if they could help someone else." They bubbled with ideas while Dan marvelled at the maturity of these girls who themselves were recipients of HCTH interventions.

When Dan talked about this project, his admiration of these girls overflowed, especially for a girl named Katy, who has been striving relentlessly to rise above her present circumstances.

She lives high up the hillside, a Manchay eyrie that takes a couple of rest stops along the pathway to reach. It is fitting, though, because Katy aims high. She's nineteen. Dan was impressed with her determination; Katy had been working nights and weekends to put together the cash, with a bit of help from HCTH, to buy the land. Now it was hers.

Dan explained that her home life appeared to be less than ideal. Her step-father, whose drinking brought beatings for her mother, lit an ambitious fire in Katy.

"I've got a lot of respect for her. She's studying industrial foods, has two jobs, and even goes to school on Saturdays," he said, a likely factor in her being chosen for the pay-forward project.

Dan gave each of the girls one hundred soles (about C$38) with the understanding that they were not to spend the money on themselves, but to help someone else. To seal the deal, Tom, Cheryl and Dan took the girls out for a celebratory chicken dinner.

Three of the pay-forward group reported their experience a year later:

- Miriam added to the inventory of a legless man who made his living selling candy on the street. She also gave money to an uncle suffering from Parkinson's disease, so he could buy medicine.

- Shirley was drawn to a poor boy who lives in the hills of Manchay and attends a Bible Club, where she helped. She took him to the centre of Lima to buy a bicycle where they were cheaper, but her thirty remaining soles were still a little short of the selling price. She dipped into her meagre savings from her part-time job to make up the difference.

- Katy focused on a family that lived near her in Manchay, a single mother with three children, including one who is disabled. Katy bought diapers for the disabled child, as well as food and other needed items.

Dan returned to Peru the following year to see how the girls were doing, and to help them in their homes. On their first trip to Peru, the Bedfords included some sight-seeing but, this time, "I was just as happy to spend my time in Manchay around the people. I really loved it."

He continued: "I was amazed at how these girls had matured in just a year. Shirley, she had a boyfriend. I thought, oh boy, we're going to lose her. Her school marks slipped, but she did a complete one-eighty... really responsible... taking turns teaching in a Bible School. We are really proud of her."

She had written a two-page letter of thanks to God, "for giving me two people so marvelous in my life as you are. I want to say to you that during the last while, my life has been changed, because I have learned to value that which is most important in this life. It is God." She also reported that she was doing well in her studies.

She now works part-time for a dentist.

Dan reflected as he told about his projects: "They say you can leave Peru, but Peru never leaves you. I like the people. They are so generous. You take them some food, and they flip it right around — the blessing is all mine they say, inviting you to share a meal."

He talked about the cramped conditions in which many live and the lack of water — laundry is done by hand in a basin. "Yet, the children are relatively clean." And with satisfaction, he said the investment by HCTH in the children, their families, and their homes is paying off.

Now he has his sights set on Africa, likely Zambia.

THE FOURNIERS

Jane and John Fournier are from Athens, Ontario. Unlike other sponsors who had a long-term connection to the Martins, their paths had only crossed three years before, when the Martins made a church presentation. "We knew it was our match."

If the Martins had a profile of likely supporters, the Fourniers would be a perfect fit. John is a recently retired nurse with a long history of working with inmates in Ontario prisons. Jane, also a health practitioner, still follows her career as a supervisor in a network of health clinics.

It was their first time following the Martins, and they were both struck by the couple's commitment. "What we didn't know was just how hands-on they worked; we didn't realize how hard they worked. We will next year, when we go back. We'll be more prepared. We'll take fewer clothes to give away and more money, so that the recipients can get exactly what they need or want," explained Jane, with John pointing out that this plan will also support the local economy. Merchants also would be helped through the purchases.

However, the Canadian visitors found happy new owners for shirts, dresses, jackets, and shoes they brought on their first trip. When they gave one girl a pair of boots, she "lit up like a Christmas tree." She had never had a pair, and her eyes shone more than the freshly polished footwear.

The Fourniers liked the Martins' approach. It motivated them, focussed them on a goal, and gave them a travel destination: "We are going to make a difference in someone's life. Maybe the change will be in our own lives," said Jane, a true philosopher and dreamer, adding that their ten-year-old son, Matt, needed to learn about the world. He would be paired with another boy his age. On the eight-hour-plus flight from Canada to Peru, young Matt chattered that the first thing he'd do upon meeting his still-unknown chum would be to ask about his favourite video game, unaware that maybe the other boy's first question might be what or whether he'd get to eat that day.

The Fourniers reflected on their ten-day visit to Peru while sitting in the dining room of their large, modern home, munching on chocolate chip cookies Matt had made. Jane said, "We anticipated that we would help the Peruvians, that we would bless them when, in fact, it was the opposite. They blessed us with their kindness and generosity. We thought we'd be taking *them* food, but three different families entertained us."

She compared the Peruvian response to the Bible's parable of the widow who made her offering of two small coins in the temple. Jesus said: "I tell you the truth, this poor widow has put more into the treasury than all the others. They all gave out of their wealth; but she, out of her poverty, put in everything — all she had to live on." (Mark 12, 43-44)

"We were giving from our abundance," Jane continued, sliding right into another example of Peruvian generosity. They had met the pastor of a local church and attended a service dedicated to missions. The congregation turned over its entire offering — about forty dollars — to the Martins, for "the poor people in Africa," and yet, they were poor themselves.

Unknown to the Fourniers as they were winging their way south, their impending arrival was causing anxiety for the Martins. Just days before, the Martins repeatedly visited the home of the boy they had chosen to pair with Matthew. Same age, bright. A perfect match. Jefferson was his name, a brother to Manuel, a high achiever in high school. The trouble was that Jefferson had gone AWOL. The Martins had wakened Manuel on the first visit, who sleepily allowed that his brother was somewhere in Lima with his grandmother. Maybe. On their second visit, Manuel was alone again. He got shifty-eyed and evasive.

So the Martins and Karina checked out the school. Jefferson had been missing from there, too. Clearly, he wasn't a candidate for HCTH sponsorship. Manuel's reticence spoke volumes; he knew from experience that sponsorship went hand-in-hand with school attendance, and Martin aid for his grandmother was unlikely without the Jefferson. It would cost her money.

Just before they left, the Martins gave Manuel a couple of shirts — a muscle shirt was a big hit — and some money to buy trousers. Normally, they would accompany him to the market, but time was short. They'd check later to ensure the purchases were made.

But the more immediate and vexing problem was that the Fourniers were primed to match Matt with Jefferson. The reaction of the Fourniers, however, put the angst to rest; there were other boys — and girls.

Juan, an eight-year-old, was hooked up with Matt and they quickly became pals, even without video games. Meanwhile, John and Jane were meeting girls already embraced by the Martins. There was Soledad, a mother and a victim of rape. "I took to her instantly," said John. "There was something about her, sad. I took her as a sponsored child. I paid for her to be enrolled in a computer program, something she had started but had to drop because of her pregnancy. Telling her she'd be able to go to classes seemed to put a spark in her eye."

He talked of the absence of home life in Canadian terms, where her father, "a gentle, humble man who we only met once," left for work early in the day and returned late at night. His kids hardly knew him. He looked across the table at his young son as he reflected on how helping Soledad helped the whole family.

There were six of them, living in a space that John estimated as about six feet by twenty, dirt floor, no beds. The Fourniers bought bunk beds which, when assembled, just left a gangway down the middle. But who's to complain, with a bed and mattress to sleep on.

That home was on their regular route in Manchay, so they stopped in often while on their rounds with the Martins.

Like John, Jane also bonded with one of the youngsters. She commented, in more general terms, that Shirley, whose home is in the mountains, "took a piece of my heart."

"We hardly ever left Manchay; we'd go in the morning, go back home for lunch, and back to Manchay for the rest of the day. Twice, though, those treks on the bus — once we tried counting the people jammed in but it was impossible — included taking Juan and Matt to the market, and another time it was to an overcrowded, seething clinic."

Jane, the nurse, had never seen anything like it. She had hoped to see a few babies, but she saw fifty. The Martins knew what lay ahead, so, for that venture, their backpacks were loaded with blankets, sleep sets and teddy bears to give away. A government program helps out these new-borns by providing cereal to the infants, but that's where the assistance ends.

There was nothing they could do, however, for the hordes of older children and adults lined up two abreast for medical attention. The state health plan, which carries with it an annual premium tied to income, covers minimal care provided by overworked staff in overcrowded facilities.

A guide told of his mother breaking her arm and waiting in line, going home and returning again, in hopes of getting treatment. In desperation, the son took her to a private clinic where he was able to get her treatment, for a fee.

It was here that another preconceived notion was set on its ear. Matt, little slight Matt, about sixty pounds soaking wet, who could pass for someone much younger, attracted much attention. The Peruvian adults worried he was malnourished.

"Here we were, thinking we were going to help them, and they thought to help us."

THE SHARONS

Sharon Mackenze and her friend Sharon Rusk, seasoned travellers, were excited as their plane from Canada touched down in Lima. The Jorge Chavez International Airport is busy, with 15 million visitors in 2013, coming in and going out on fifty-seven different airlines. As airports go, it was an inviting place, listed as the best South American airport for years running. But their excitement gave way to growing anxiety; Cesar, the cab driver booked to meet them, wasn't there, and they didn't know where they were going.

"Two women, travelling alone…we were unsure of what to do. We were getting concerned," admitted Sharon, but at least she could speak Spanish.

Beyond the airport doors was a world that lacked the sense of security the airport interior offered. A horde of travel guides, taxi drivers, and hotel chauffeurs were waving signs with names on them. None had Mackenzie or Rusk, or Sharon One or Sharon Two, on them. More and more travellers disappeared, lugging bags off to waiting cars, but still no Cesar. They fretted; should they dare to hire a taxi? But to where? They watched the diminishing crowd with fading hope.

Thirty minutes later Cesar, the cab driver the Martins commissioned to pick up HCTH visitors, arrived to take them to the mission house that they'd call home for the next two weeks. They didn't query the delay, and were just glad to be in the relative safety of his well-used car, as he zigged, zagged, braked, and accelerated through the maze of bumper-to-bumper traffic.

Any anxiety, either with the wait or the wild car ride, evaporated in the boisterous greetings, laughter, and hugs, as bags filled with clothing brought for the Martin charges rolled over the concrete walkway and bounced up the stairs to the second storey apartment.

The apartment itself is modern, although somewhat spartan by North American standards. The daily rate for guests is only enough to cover costs and meet the HCTH objective of "paying your own way."

The Martins are people-people, genuinely. It doesn't matter, it seems, whether it is in social conversation, in a presentation, in the field, or upon arrival of a house guest — their pleasure at social interaction draws people. Their openness is a gift to the stream of supporters coming to experience their world.

The Martins arrange the basic logistics for their visitors — someone will meet their flight and get them to their lodging

— but beyond that, they're on their own. And, once settled, the Martins follow their own schedule. Follow along, if you like, get involved in some project, if you like, or go sight-seeing; although most visitors want to be directly engaged.

In some cases, it starts by seeing what happens to the extra bags visitors bring to augment the clothes and gifts the Martins brought themselves for distribution. Like the Martins, they, too, had tried to stay within — and sometimes bend — airline luggage regulations. The visitors are sort of God's "mules," to borrow a word from a less honourable business, transporting clothes and toys to be given to local people.

Following the Martins means lots of interaction with local people, a rich addition to the experience of visiting a new country. The Martins enable visitors to see the country from the inside, not just peering through the tourist lens. For the Sharons, it was visiting homes and schools. However, they warned another prospective Peru visitor: "If you are going to follow Tom, beware. When he says he's leaving at eight-thirty, you better be ready, because he will be at the door at eight."

They bubble with enthusiasm about their time in Lima. "You walk a lot, it's hilly … very vigorous … the people are lovely … sweet, generous …" The Sharons are trim and fit, as one would expect from a pair of experienced hikers; traipsing up and down the hillsides only fed their enthusiasm for what they were doing.

Their primary task was to help in a daycare, a facility owned by Kids Alive. It was enclosed by a high brick fence with access vetted by a guard. Several classrooms for different age groups surround a well-equipped but small play area. The nursery is a focal point for visitors, where the slightly older children nap on mats on the floor, oblivious to classmates stepping over them. Stacks of small bunks, cage-like structures, built into the wall are for the youngest. Those enclosures wouldn't pass muster in Canada, but are cozy "bassinettes" for happily sleeping infants.

Staff, both paid and volunteer, are caring and watchful, particularly at meal time. The Martins sometimes lunch with the students and staff. One day, Tom felt that, while the food was good, something in the serving seemed chewy. "I had stopped eating it even before they told me [the chewy parts] were intestines. The kids ate our share and really liked it." They ate at the orphanage often during their time in Peru, and the fare was never again quite so exotic, leaning toward the Peruvian staples of beans and vegetables.

The Sharons, who missed out on the intestines, were assigned to a group of four-year-olds; their duties included trips to a zoo and to a medical clinic to leave medical supplies and baby blankets.

While the daycare area is the primary focus of the Kids Alive facility, skills training is also offered to adults. In one area, a group of women — several with their children in daycare — was learning sewing skills, making items for sale in the market. In another area, work progressed on an ad hoc basis where volunteers were building more classrooms as money became available.

Neither Sharon mentioned "an interesting day" that Tom highlighted in an email — a trip from the daycare back to base when they encountered a road block. "There were at least two hundred policemen. Some were on horseback, many with plastic shields, with guns and rifles, armoured vehicles, etc. We got out of the bus to walk the last little way into Manchay. Supposedly there were criminals living in some of the houses." No more details, never mentioned again.

"The highlight was visiting the home of a young mother named Karina. [Karina is a common name here, one shared with the HCTH local representative] We told her that Sharon wanted to sponsor her little boy Esteban. Karina and Sharon both cried."

This Karina was about the same age as the girls Dan Bedford had inspired with the pay-forward idea, and had been invited to the chicken dinner with the girls. Tom said "it was especially good for Karina" to be part of the group, since her husband had just left her. She lived alone in a small house of thin veneer, on the roof of the home of her parents, with three-year-old Esteban.

Sharon Mackenzie said, "I felt a little shy at first [meeting families in their homes] because you don't want to make them feel embarrassed [about the obvious difference between wealthy visitors and their own state of poverty], but that's just not important to them."

Sharon Rusk jumps in with an example of being invited to one home for dinner. Two children of this family are sponsored by HCTH. The hosts draped the room with white sheets, lit candles, decorated for Christmas — sort of like a small, intimate Italian restaurant. "They didn't have much, but they were saying that the visit was something special."

The torrent slows. "I love those people."

Sharon Mackenzie adds, "They are lovely, and so generous. Out of what they have, they share." A major disappointment was that her plans to return in 2014 fell through.

KIRSTEN HOLLETT

Sixteen-year-old Kirsten Hollett clutched a photograph of the people who, she had been assured, would be waiting in Lusaka to collect her after her twenty-hour, two-stage trip from Canada. It was a hot, humid night, and it was late. The arrival area was jostling and noisy, a typical scene in a large metropolitan airport which 800,000 people pass through each year. Many of them were there that night, so it seemed.

Homemade cardboard signs waved in the air, the typical link the world-over between travellers and their local connection.

"I was pretty nervous, it was sort of nerve racking." Slowly scanning the field of signs, Kirsten's heart gave a little jump when she spotted her name and recognized her hosts, whom she had only met through email. Relief and excitement made for an enthusiastic greeting, everyone talking at once, with lots of nervous laughter. The couple was the Mfulas, who were close friends — actually partners of sorts — of the Martins.

Lusaka, the capital of Zambia, has a population of about 1.8 million, mostly English speaking, making it somewhat bigger than Canada's capital of Ottawa. The city appeared pretty bleak and foreboding in the middle of the night to Kirsten.

Cyrus and Prisca Mfula took her to their modern house in a compound that was protected by a high concrete wall topped with barbed wire. Security is a preoccupation in much of Africa and South America; robbery is a common business, although Kirsten was never molested.

"I went because I wanted to help people and it was a way to get community service hours. It wasn't a mission trip," she explained, although the link with the Martins was through the Roblin Wesleyan Church in Napanee, which they all attended.

The morning after her arrival, Kirsten accompanied her hosts to church, and they showed her around so that she could get adjusted.

She met many members of her hosts' family, beginning with their two children. Lunch was sausages and chips. Then, it was off by bus to Choma, the Zambian base for the Martins. If you bought a ticket at Lusaka, you got a seat. Otherwise, along the route all the way to the end of the line, getting a seat would be a tossup. Even getting on at all was no sure thing. Getting that seat depended on the total load and the ability of bus attendants to shoulder more people — some with chickens and other belongings — into what appears to be non-existent space.

The four-hour trip to Choma seemed long to Kirsten, given the proximity with other travellers and the rapidly deteriorating roads as Lusaka faded in the mirrors. She counted the endless potholes and watched the towns, mostly dreary, slipping by.

Choma was "a pretty rundown town" in the eyes of a Canadian girl. The commercial district had small shops with worn out signs. Dirt roads were the norm, from which vehicles kicked up clouds of reddish dust.

A Zambia Travel Guide listed the usual businesses found in most small towns, but highlights "a super little museum" and a large supermarket "with a good variety of fresh and frozen food." The Guide's authors felt that ginger cake and freshly baked bread were worthy of praise. North of town, visitors may find charcoal sellers and local fishermen waving fresh fish, trying to gain attention from passing motorists.

The town itself, in some respects, was like urban areas everywhere, with the mixture of wealth and poverty, of enterprise and idleness, of twenty-first century satellite dishes and destitution. In the poorer areas, such as Mwapona, even an old television set was an oddity. By North American standards, it was impoverished.

Wide streets featured vehicles of all vintages, extended cab trucks, rickety 1940s models. Bicycles were everywhere and were a desirable commodity. Kirsten's quarters were in a guest house, the Martins' base, in the small compound close to the Pilgrim Wesleyan Church.

She spent most of her time working with children in an orphanage started years ago by a German couple. At least eleven of the sixty children are HIV positive, including one girl whose father died of AIDS last year, and whose mother is HIV positive. Many had been given a death sentence at birth by their parents. Kirsten talked of one boy with open sores.

Most of the kids were shy and wary at the outset, a watchfulness that quickly dissipated as they were caught up in Kirsten's stories. "I really liked them, they were good kids. Happy smiles … [they] seemed happy with what they had."

The youngest child was nine. The oldest was Kirsten's age. They could read, "but they really struggled, and I would help them for six or seven hours a day." She'd colour pictures with those too sick to play soccer, or were just disinterested in it; Kirsten didn't play soccer either.

Shopping expeditions with Cheryl and girls being sponsored were fun times for Kirsten — just imagine a clutch of teenagers turned loose in a market. The trips involved buying clothes and personal items for Beatrice and Ruth on one day, a girl named Beauty on another.

In the evenings, she'd unwind by reading, making bracelets, or playing cards with the Martins.

She bought a bicycle so that she could accompany the Martins on their rounds. When one person went into a shop, another would always have to stand guard over the coveted bicycles. She gave hers to one of her new-found friends when she returned to Canada.

One of the families she visited often during her two weeks in Zambia included a three-year-old charmer named Colin. His mother sold charcoal, vegetables, and "other things" from her home. When Kirsten came over to read and coach his nine- and thirteen-year-old sisters, he stuck to her like a burr. He was ready for kindergarten.

Although HCTH sponsored the other four members of the family in school, there was no money left, either in the HCTH account or in the family, to start him off.

"He is the same age as my nephew," Kirsten observed as she fretted about him, "and was being left behind." She told the Martins of her concern, and they were able to assign a sponsor for him.

It is hard to say who was the principal beneficiary of her two weeks in Zambia, Kirsten herself, or any one the children she spent time with; likely it would be a draw, but it is safe to speculate that those two weeks were a life-changing experience for her.

Chapter 16
Tom's Banking Career

"THEY ALSO SERVE WHO STAND AND WAIT."

Banking in Africa is a challenge for the Martins but a necessary part of their style of financial stewardship. It is often frustrating, and sometimes even entertaining. It goes with being responsible for the supporters' donations.

Most weekday mornings when they are in Uganda or Zambia, Tom goes to the bank. Then, on almost as many mornings, he heads off to school. It is an essential ritual brought about by the unpredictability of the banking system, matched by the unpredictable demands of the schools, students, and families.

At the end of the day, his wallet is pretty thin, maybe empty, needing to be replenished come morning — if wire and bank transfers were successful — and he'll have more stories of how money was distributed

His banking accounts bring to mind Stephen Leacock's *My Banking Career*, in which he writes "When I go into a bank, I get rattled. The clerks rattle me …." Tom doesn't get rattled, but the possibilities of unexpected circumstances makes him anxious, and he'd be less than human if he didn't get impatient.

Fortunately on occasion there are distractions, such as watching a guard chase a rat across the floor, corner it, and dispatch it with his shoe. The event would also kill some time, along with the rat — Tom waited thirty minutes the day of the great rat hunt, time enough to compare the guard's technique with his own, since he had broken a broom handle in a personal rat encounter at home.

Rats aside, there are other realities in African banking that any customer from North America needs to learn. The building might look like a bank, smell like a bank, and have even some of the enhancements of modern day bank branches, such as ATMs. But service can be quite another matter, and it generally comes at the end of a long lineup.

Timing is important. Tom learned quickly, if at all possible to avoid going early Mondays, late Fridays, or at noon on any day.

Sometimes, though, Tom does not have a choice — if, for example, he's responsible for children who can't get into school until their fees are paid. Carrying large sums of money is risky in Africa, as it is everywhere, but is made worse by the sheer volume of the actual currency; in Uganda, an American dollar converts into about 2,500 shillings.

There are times when cash in hand is absolutely essential for unexpected expenses. In Kampala, the Martins' driver was stopped by a police officer, possibly because there was a white person in the car. Shillings, ten thousand of them — amounting to about four dollars — solved the problem, whatever it was.

There is also the worry that when Tom reaches the teller, he'll be told the bank is out of money or, worse, there is no money in their account. The Martins remember the year when the transferred money had simply disappeared and did not appear in the bank records for ten days. Which raises another concern: the possibility of insider theft.

Joram, the Martins' agent in Uganda, caught discrepancies once in the HCTH bank statements which added up to about $6,000. Somebody was skimming. The teller with sticky fingers lost his job and, eventually, the bank made good on the losses.

Leacock may have been rattled by his encounter but, for the Martins, there's resigned acceptance. There are ATMs, a shortcut to service *when they work*; but the causes of their unreliability are legion. Most common is that the bank has run out of cash. They must wait for the next delivery from Kampala. Maybe tomorrow.

"I went to the ATM and on the fifth time, I finally got money. I had to go into the bank to take some out. I hate doing this because of the time." Once, a trusted student was commissioned by the Martins to make the bank trip on their behalf during the traditionally busy time. It took two hours.

Then there are the unpredictable times, when the teller is busy telling a hilarious story to a friend as the anxious patrons wait. Locals know the drill, waiting is routine in their lives. The story ends and the line leans forward, then sways back as the teller puts up the 'closed' card in the window and heads off on a break. Some patrons leave, others roll their eyes and settle in for a wait of who-knows-how-long.

But sometimes, the stars are aligned: "I was second in line. I withdrew five million Ugandan shillings, or about $2,000."

The bank visits are only a part of what the Martins see as responsible stewardship. In some cases, it is to ensure that money earmarked for school fees gets to its predetermined destination. In others, it is to confirm that the sponsored child is, in fact, attending school, and that the money is credited to the child's account. And, finally, it gives the old school teacher an opportunity to assess the schools himself, which often have signs with innovative spellings, such as, "If you do not use English, you will be penelised" or "attend classes approprietly."

The wrinkles in the school interactions are creative. On top of the basic fees, some schools offer additional classes which cost extra, of course, but possibly come with better spelling.

Clothes and supplies are also expenses that rely on Tom's trips to the bank. One child said she had asked her father to buy a pencil, but he refused because he had no money. Of course, he had money for beer. Her explanation may have been unusual, but was a variation on the demands that regularly set the Martins off to the market, where they are steady customers for school supplies, shoes and uniforms. After, of course, they have been to the bank.

Chapter 17
Empowerment

"NEVER BE AFRAID TO TRUST AN UNKNOWN
FUTURE TO A KNOWN GOD."

— Corrie Ten Boom

Wisdom is a coveted commodity that underpins the goals of their work. Cheryl explained early on that, "We find, with families, that we need to empower them so that they can help themselves, so that we are not going back every year to help them. We want them to be able to buy their own food and pay their own school fees, but the only way you can help them is to give them land so that they can grow their own crops, or help them start a business."

Two realities collided, and a twenty-hour plane ride in the economy section, plus airport time, offered a lot of time to mull them over. The first was considering who might benefit most — which families, which children — that raised the second reality, "We can't help them all."

A typical arrival: when the plane lands, the Martins hit the ground running.

Whether it is Uganda or Zambia, news of their arrival travels fast. A drum beat in rural areas is the community PA system.

However the word gets around, the locals arrive even before the Martins have unpacked a single suitcase. There are three groups, mainly — friends to welcome them back, friends with financial needs, and others who simply hope that their ship has come in.

Within hours, Tom had paid school fees for several children. More people and issues bubbled to the surface. Some families wanted their children to change schools; students were in dire need of school supplies; others wanted a better place to live. When the last one left, sleep came quickly, despite time zones, and dawn seemed to come extra early the next day.

In both countries, the first imperative is buying bags of rice, maize, and sugar for quick distribution to families they know are destitute.

"What a day Wednesday was. We borrowed Patrick Walusimbi's large truck. We bought nine 50kg bags of rice and nine 50kg bags of beans. We also bought one goat and eight small pigs. We then delivered them to the orphanage and eight homes of the poor. We also bought blankets, kerosene lamps, and jugs of kerosene."

There was no mention of how those purchases fit into the back-of-the-envelope budget except that available funds are finite. The Martins, however, have great faith in out-of-the-blue donations to pay for out-of-the-blue requirements.

Reliance on divine interventions, however, also requires "feet on the ground" to translate them into appropriate action. The Martins do feel, however, that divine interventions often guide the decisions they are forced to make every day about which people they can help, and with what.

Helping children through school and into university, is explicitly clear in the HCTH mandate. So is helping the poor, which takes many forms but, in the context of empowerment, the most possibilities lie in agricultural endeavours.

In the earliest days of HCTH, becoming a landowner in Africa wasn't even considered. Now, Tom's thoughts turn to how crops are growing, how many people now are sharecroppers, what new opportunities exist. A new fish pond and solar panels in Zambia, more pigs and goats in Uganda are on the agenda.

These material matters, however, are secondary; when he is back in Canada his thoughts swing more to the people. Even though email exchanges are frequent, there are those too young, or too poor to participate in these exchanges. So his thoughts alternate between remembering and wondering.

On the ground, the speculation gives way to reality.

"Today started out early. I rode to Namakozi to meet Barbara and Viola at eight a.m. to go to the garden to plant beans, maize, and cassava. We got about 25 percent of the garden planted. Cheryl had to stay home, because Sulah was coming to fix our eaves troughs.

"We worked in the garden until about 10:30. I then rushed home to bathe, and then went to deliver food to families. We give food monthly to nine poor families. This goes on even when we are not here. The families are very appreciative.

"I had to go to the bank. It took fifty-five minutes.

"I had to go back to Pride S.S. today because Noreen needed a new uniform … We had a nice visit from a lady from Tennessee in the afternoon … Around supper time we usually get our visitors. Tonight we had three. Winnie needed a calculator for school. The carpenter came to ask if we needed any work done. Then Sulah came … two students who just finished high school are taking computer classes, which is good for them.

"I gave money to Dennis for his last term of university. It will be nice to see him finished."

It is an agenda that plays out daily, the small events which, in their own way, help propel individuals and groups toward an education, a healthier life, and, ultimately, self-sufficiency. Over the eleven years of Martin interventions, there have been a host of remarkable transformations, many of which started as simply as planting beans.

HCTH owns property in both Uganda and Zambia and selects both families and individuals who can benefit from the use of the land, rent-free. They keep what they grow, but sometimes chickens and vegetables turn up at the Martins' door with no explanation.

The process of selecting people for garden plots appears haphazard, like the driving force behind all of the Martin decisions. Generally, they respond to indicators drawn from their connection with the individuals: their need, motivation, and reliability. They also gather intelligence from their trusted friends, who are often the local clergy. For the farms, the recipients also need to be able to work in harmony with others.

In many cases, however, the interventions are specific to individuals.

Irene, a widow in Zambia, is a mother of four who lived in a dilapidated single-room shanty that she rented for nine dollars a month. She was there because she could no longer live with her mother in the village, far from her work. One mattress for her and her daughter. Her sons slept on the floor; they'd never had a mattress, never slept on a bed. The Martins got them mattresses and arranged to have beds built, while, at the same time, helped Irene develop her business. Her enterprise involved buying cloth in large lots and selling it in smaller amounts in the nearby villages, a venture that was working moderately well, although all her travel was by foot, bringing the bolts of cloth home and walking her sales route.

While she was industrious, she was also poor, and became even poorer one day when thieves broke into her home, ransacked it, and cleaned out her meagre cash reserves.

"Why would they steal from me, [one] of the poorest?" she asked, and no one knew the answer. But the Martins had a response. They built her a house.

She had been knocked flat by the theft, but was revived by the gift of a home and is flourishing again, better than ever. She used to walk the two miles or so to her market place but, in 2014, when the Martins left Zambia, they gave her Cheryl's bike. Meanwhile, thanks to a couple of Canadian women who had met her earlier, two of her children are in school and are set up through high school.

Another woman, Susan, had to borrowed clothes to go to church when the Martins first met her. A year later, she was lending clothes to others. How had it happened? HCTH had helped her get started in a business that was successful enough that, within a year, she was helping others in straits as dire as hers has been.

One fellow whose connection with HCTH started in school and who now flourishes in the adult world of Choma, is Susan's son, Nchimunya. He is the third oldest of nine born to Susan, the second of his father's five wives. The number of half-siblings is uncertain. Nchimunya would watch the other kids go to school. For him, he only got a taste, Grade One, before the money ran out.

But his brief introduction only served to create a thirst for education. He longed to go, and, even as a youngster, he had a special spark and an agile mind. Nchimunya told the headmaster that he would work for him if he'd allow him to attend classes. It sounded like a make-work project, but Nchimunya could attend Grade Two classes if he built a grass fence around the headmaster's property. In Grade Three, the deal was to care for the garden. Grade Four was more of the same.

The Martins met Nchimunya when he was in Grade Five. In typical Martin fashion, they went to his home, taking in the one-room dwelling with its leaky roof and single blanket for the kids. Also in typical Martin fashion, Tom invited Nchimunya to accompany him to the market, where they bought the family a large bag of corn flour. Chatting on the way, Tom learned that Nchimunya's name means the second child born less than a year after the older sibling of the same sex, and it applies equally to boys and girls.

"I didn't realize the impact our visits would have on his life," Tom recalled, as he recounted the daily visits to the home for the next month. A sponsor was found for Nchimunya's school fees through Grade Nine, and another agreed to pay for a two-year trade school program, where he learned construction skills as a builder, electrician, plumber and bricklayer.

In 2013, Nchimunya wrote, "Great thanks once again to the tools Graham bought for me. With a few that I bought, they've made a difference in terms of doing the work … small machineries (sic) because of my level and thinking capacity of trying to cast my net wider."

Nchimunya's ruminations, which he shares wistfully, never stop. In one breath, he tells of his longings, and the next about a client who has "one of the small machineries" he covets. Maybe he could work for it.

"It is my great desire to have them, because that is where the construction industry is held." And, not only that but, if he owned those small machineries, they could be rented to others at an hourly rate. In any event, he had drawn plans for a house he was building, which he would be sending on to a prospective client.

He is designing houses, using AUTOCAD on a computer he borrows from a friend. He'd really like a cement mixer, which costs about $2,500, and a vibrator ($500) which would enable him to make good, solid floors in far less time. And a computer ($300) would be helpful, because he's off to Lusaka to take an upgrading course in AUTOCAD.

"It is my great desire to have them, because ... as you know, a tool being a device that allows to do one's work easier." That might not be quite as big a revelation as he may have thought.

The Martins did give him Cheryl's bike after he told them about his ninety-minute walk, each way to work. Tom then walked from Mityana into Choma to buy her a replacement.

Nchimunya exemplifies the Martin way of operating, whether it is distributing food, selecting children for school, or monitoring micro businesses. Once a family, a student, a child is caught up in their network, the Martins don't abandon them as long as they are making an effort, even after they have met their educational goal or gained their wings in the entrepreneurial world.

While HCTH had helped Nchimunya get the education and skills to be a construction contractor, Sulah's needs were different. He had carpentry skills, but lacked tools. No tools, no work, until the Martins embraced him and his family more than a decade ago.

Raised a Muslim, Sulah converted to Christianity in 2006.

A HCTH supporter bought him the tools, and Tom kept his eyes open for jobs that fit Sulah's capabilities: building beds, tables and doing house repairs. It was a small jump from those types of projects to houses, including one for his own growing family. He proudly reported to his sponsor that he was no longer living in a one-room dwelling with his wife and three children, that they had a garden on HCTH land, and that his children now were in school, paving the way to possibilities that he never had.

The individual successes are varied, sometimes creative, but always practical.

David finished high school after being sponsored for several years. Now, on the threshold of a career, he wants to sell peanut flour in the market, just like his father did, using the machine his father had to grind the peanuts. HCTH helped him.

Amos made bricks, twenty thousand of them, but had no money to buy firewood to cure them. A donor provided the cash and, with the income from the sale of the bricks, Amos could complete his last semester of college and realize his dream of becoming a teacher.

One account from Uganda, selected at random, reinforces an implicit hope that the Martins' efforts will bring some lasting benefit: chickens, cows, goats, and even rabbits all have greater potential than just the making of tomorrow's dinner. A Canadian family gave the Martins money for a cow, which went to the home of a girl who was sponsored in her last year of high school — the first in her extended family to have attained that level of education. They'd be able to have — and sell — milk, by the cup. Then, there were fifty chicks bought to replace a flock that had been purchased the previous year. Sold or eaten? Either way, they were gone.

"We explained to the lady that it was necessary to keep some of the birds to build the flock for the future," Tom said, without recrimination. Otherwise, they'd be eating their future.

Some understand the concept. "I have found two families with pigs to sell," Tom said, adding proudly that HCTH had got them started in the business. Now, he was looking for an appropriate market, explaining they like to buy from people in their network.

Money for these purchases came from gift certificates, bought by supporters and entrusted to the Martins to use as they see fit. At the time of writing, the Martins had enough money to buy more than forty pigs and goats. Tom was probably smiling when he reported here that they had provided ten goats and two pigs to a family, who then sold them to buy a cow. "This is how pigs and goats become cows — only in Africa."

Isaac's leap to self-sufficiency began on a plane when Tom struck up a conversation with a couple who lived in Canada, but were working as auditors for an international accountancy firm in Romania. They were mesmerized by Tom's accounts of HCTH activities among children blocked from school by the lack of money.

Somehow, Isaac cropped up in the conversation, just like dozens of other kids do whenever Tom can find an audience. Tom and the accountants exchanged addresses, and only days later, the Martins received an email, saying the new-found friends wanted to send Isaac to university, and funds were on the way.

Isaac is a law clerk now in Mityana, handling real estate and financial matters. A life he could never have even dreamt about before HCTH.

Chapter 18
The Open Door

"FAMILIES ARE MADE IN THE HEART."
— C. JoyBell C

Down through the years, Tom has told audiences everywhere that the people they touch are "like family to us, our children, our grandchildren." His emails provide a picture of a proud patriarch and matriarch surveying the family that seems to grow with regularity and diverse intentions.

Night after night, beginning at about five p.m., people arrive at the Martin doorstep to visit, ask for help, leave a gift of fruit, and then leave but not necessarily quickly. The sponsored students stay to visit, chattering about both their achievements and needs, while playing cards and eating popcorn. Typically, they head home for the evening meal, which may be rice and peanut sauce provided by HCTH, at about nine or nine-thirty.

The Martins know the culture, so, whenever possible, their own evening meal is slotted in before the visitors begin to arrive. The scheduling does not always work, with guests, oblivious of the cultural differences, drifting in at five p.m., six p.m., nine p.m. Somewhat resigned, Tom explains "They eat late here," as his stomach longs for an equivalent of a six p.m. dinner after the catch-as-catch-can lunch of maybe a bun and soft drink.

Two girls, mentioned fondly and frequently by the Martins, are often among the early arrivals. They really don't count as guests as they often work hand-in-glove with the Martins: cooking a meal, cleaning the house, working in the garden beside Tom. They are family, after all. Generally, if one has kids, the kids have to pitch in and help, don't they? And, if they live away, they are welcomed whenever they show up. That's just the way it is — at least for the Martins — but, in fact, any visitor gets the same kind of warm welcome.

Such activities give daily testimony to the Martins' conviction that we are all equal partners in God's universe. Whatever the colour of the skin, the blood is red and the sweat on the brow is the same.

James is a young man from the Congo who has been living on HCTH land for three years and is doing well. His candor one day illustrated how shy, wary young people gain confidence as they are embraced by the Martins. It doesn't take them long, in the Martins' kitchen, for fear to melt away as they talk, dream and share their heartaches.

James got right to the point. He is lonely, he said, and asked for prayer that he would get a job that would allow him to buy a wife.

"This is the first time we have been asked to pray for this issue," Tom remarks.

In all, there are seventy-nine in the Martins' Zambian "family," fifteen with no parents, forty-eight with one parent, with the rest having two parents who provide limited degrees of interest and support. Mentioned most frequently, though, are kids the Martins have snatched from either extreme poverty or worse, such as Maria. She was another house girl, burdened with chores, and worse, with no opportunity to go to school.

"It is sad what humans will do to their own kind," says Tom.

When money is available — and sometimes when dollars need to be stretched — it is an easy call to rescue a Maria, drawing her into their network. Other decisions are more difficult. A girl was performing poorly in school. The Martins encouraged her to transfer to vocational training, but ran into stiff resistance from her mother. Her Grade Eleven marks were poor, "and we told her [that] even if she found a school to take her onto Grade Twelve, we would not pay for her because she does not have the ability." They offered to pay vocational training fees. The mother's response was unreported.

Another mother came to the gate with her son, Solomon, looking for money for school fees. His name had been Sulah, but his Christian mother changed it to Solomon when he was confirmed in the Anglican Church. His Muslim father said that if she took him to a Christian church, "then their God will have to look after him," including school fees.

Only once in a multi-year log of emails does a hint of exasperation creep into the message, when Tom said in an email, that, finally, they would have an evening off.

"Oh no, I just heard Cheryl welcoming someone at the gate."

Chapter 19
Motorcycle Diaries, Martin Style

"THE REPAIR SHOP IS A SECOND HOME
FOR OWNERS OF OLD MOTORCYCLES."

The Ugandan motorcycle is a Chinese 125 CC model, bought by the Martins in 2006. Nearly ten years later, it was still bouncing over and around potholes, with as many as three (small) passengers and their groceries on the back. It doesn't have a name, which seems a bit unfortunate, given its frequent and prominent appearances in the Martin emails from Uganda. But it does have a reputation.

Tom says travelling the roads on the motorcycle, or taxis called *boda-bodas*, is the most dangerous part of their mission work in Uganda. The bike's redeeming feature, however, is that it can make the treks up and down the hills easier, especially in light of the unscheduled and frequent requests for help from their "family," who live over a wide area.

Each time the Martins return to Uganda, there is a worry mixed with the excitement of coming back — will the motorcycle start? And if it starts, will it run? Will the tires be flat? Blistering temperatures play havoc with motorized vehicles left idle for long periods.

They rely on that motorcycle for so much, doing chores, getting supplies, but mostly for making house calls to their eclectic constituency whose one common element is that wherever they live, it's a rough and dirty road to get there.

So, slotted right in there with airing out the house and cleaning up the accumulated dust is the business of riding — or pushing — the bike to the mechanic.

"Thank you for your prayers about the motorcycle," Tom wrote just after they arrived. "It started… we took it to the repair man to get it tuned up. It needed a new battery."

The thankfulness was short lived. It stalled again, and no amount of tinkering got it going again. Like so many other times, it had to be pushed to the repair shop

"[The mechanic] said come back in one hour. I came back in three hours and it still wasn't done. He said thirty more minutes. I came back two hours later and it was done," said Tom. After sixteen trips to Uganda over ten years, he understands local work habits and generally fits in side trips to make use of available time.

On one of those trips, Tom was intercepted by a friend who said his bicycle needed to be repaired, "so we stopped at the bike repair man to arrange that. He gave us five avocados. I gave him a hat."

The description of the bike, its usefulness, its fits of reliability and unreliability, frequent repairs, and periodic contrariness is reminiscent of the movie *Motorcycle Diaries,* which recounts the life of Ernesto "Che" Guevara, whose early years included continent-wide travel on a temperamental old motorcycle. Over and over again, Guevara and his friend picked themselves up from the dirt, pushed the bike to a mechanic who would get it going again, sometimes using only a pair of pliers and fence wire.

That's the bike part, but the journey itself changed Guevara from an aspiring medical student into an internationally known Marxist guerilla, a transformation brought about by the injustices he witnessed on his trek among the poor. Except for the Marxist bit, it resonates with what the Martins do for individuals, albeit on a much smaller scale.

For those who can afford them, small motorcycles are the chosen mode of transportation in many parts of Africa and Asia. In Hanoi, we witnessed an amazing sight — a forest of waving kumquat trees scooting along the crowded thoroughfares, each perched on the frame of a motor bike, along with a family of as many as five, clinging on for dear life. (Kumquat trees are an essential in Vietnamese New Year's celebrations.) Commonplace were motorcycles with a couple of hapless pigs, hog-tied of course, strapped on each side on their one-way trip to market.

Tom has his own stories. He was at the repair shop — a second home for owners of old bikes — when he heard a commotion in the street. A small crowd ran past with a covey of motor bikes in the vanguard. There had been a murder and, because the police did not attend the scene of the crime, the folks were taking the body to the police station. "Being laid out" took on new meaning for the onlookers with the mostly covered corpse, lying on a board, tied horizontally across the back of the bike.

This spectacle might have been the most unusual, but a bike loaded with what looked like a whole living room was more impressive. A chesterfield and chair perched precariously, overhanging the front, sides and back of the motorcycle, dwarfing the driver who crouched low, peering out from between two chesterfield legs.

Public taxi service is offered by *boda-bodas*, a vehicle on which the back wheel of a motorcycle is replaced by an axle and a wheel at each end, basically creating motorized tricycles. They are as ubiquitous as they are hair-raising. (North Americans riding them might want to ensure their insurance is paid up.) In the Martins' opinion they are dangerous, not because of their design, but because of the drivers. Many seem to have been trained as Kamikaze pilots, as they dart through holes in traffic that open miraculously in the nick of time and close just as fast. When Tom writes about taking a *boda-boda*, he usually includes a request that readers pray for safety.

Locals, however, have a different perspective. The Martins have a standing order — paid for by a Canadian donor — for a *boda-boda* to take a disabled woman to church each Sunday. Occasionally, a student facing an eight-kilometre walk home from a meeting is grateful for a ride in a *boda-boda*. And, when necessary, Tom uses them himself — with trepidation.

His own motorcycle experiences he dismisses — once he was flung off his bike, cracking his helmet — with a cryptic "I had an accident." He was more concerned about an elderly woman who had fallen off a *boda-boda* near the Martin home. "She was hurt, but we are not sure how bad. It looked like she was coming home from church. She had a long dress on. Sometimes [dresses] get caught in the chain of the motorcycle..."

He goes on: "We never feel unsafe [in Uganda], except on the streets," casually mentioning incidents of roadway mayhem, such as when someone drove into the side of their rented car. He speaks, with tongue in cheek, about orderly traffic in places such as Toronto, New York, or Chicago, and longs for the tranquility of the back roads around Napanee.

Driving when it is raining is a daunting prospect because "the roads are disastrous." He tries to make his trips in the morning due to the frequency of afternoon downpours, and because rain also affects the motorcycle's disposition. It balks at getting wet, often leaving Tom to push it home.

But their motorbike, however sulky or untrustworthy, helps them cover a lot of ground in one day, much more than they could manage on foot.

"There was a lot of running around today. I took the motorcycle to Central High School to visit Sylvia and Annet. I later visited Sylvia's family and bought items for her mother to sell in her shop. I took Sylvia and her sister Jacklin and brother Shafic to the market to buy needed school items. I visited the eleven girls from a girl's home. Two of the girls are sponsored through HCTH, [and] one of their sponsors sent money to buy the girls a treat. I will visit again later. I then visited a family nearby which is helped by HCTH in the family business and with sponsored children."

No breakdowns that day, but every trip has an edge of uncertainty, with ending up walking always a distinct possibility. His philosophical accounts can be appreciated by anyone with experience with old(er) motorcycles or bicycles. They understand the patience that comes with ownership, and the appreciation of a close relationship with a mechanic. It has a broken weld, it doesn't start, the tires are beyond repair — it happens. Nothing to get upset about, just a bit of juggling of the schedule.

In Zambia, where their constituency is more concentrated, the travel mode of choice for the Martins is bicycle. Each year, they buy two new ones, ride them for a season, and give them away when they leave. "Used bikes are pretty rare. If they are good, people want to keep them. If they are not, we don't want them either."

They have given away more than twenty bikes, which cost about one hundred dollars each, over the years of their Zambian visits. Added to that number are others simply purchased for individuals who have long distances to travel or, as in the case of a street merchant, to help him make his rounds.

Only one of those bicycles has come to an unhappy end. The Martins gave one to a student because she lived far from her school; they told her to keep it safe, because it was Cheryl's bike, and she'd want it back the following year.

A few months later, a sheepish and sorrowful email arrived to say it had been stolen.

In an early-days email, Tom remarked that locals laughed to see Cheryl riding a bicycle. Women didn't do that, and Cheryl's long skirt made it more of a spectacle. Now, her trips around town no longer rate a second glance.

In Lima, the Martins rely on public transit, which gives Tom a glorious opportunity to befriend any little kid on its mother's knee or, indeed, any adult jammed armpit to armpit in the buses ferrying passengers to and from the dozens of slums that circle the city.

Besides the driver, each bus comes with a ticket taker — *cobradors*, from the Spanish word that means "to collect." He

—it is usually a male — has a complicated job in that fares vary with the drop off spots along the route. On each of our several trips, I was in awe at his skills. He has to remember which passenger has paid, which isn't much of a challenge during off hours, but, to an uneducated eye, is an amazing exercise at peak times. He herds, prods and pushes more and more people onto the bus with Spanish encouragement of "back, back" while hanging onto the open door as the bus hurtles off to its next stop. If he can, he'll squeeze among the passengers to collect fares. Otherwise, he'll catch them as they dismount. At times like that, it is good to have the cash clutched in hand; it could be risky trying to reach into a pocket, because that pocket may belong to someone else.

The ride is an exhilarating experience if you are with a knowledgeable companion as a guide, but daunting if left to figure it out on your own: no apparent route signs on the buses and no posted fares, let alone knowing how the fares are collected, or if the bus will stop at your destination. Offsetting the potential for anxiety is the pleasure of watching the Peruvians interact with the driver, the ticket taker, and each other. It is a picture of civility and — it appears, at least —honesty, which is enviable.

Without a fuss, elderly travellers are given seats, never mind how challenging it is to clear a path to it. Cheryl's white hair stands her in good stead; Tom, not so much since his baseball cap hides his hair.

When the bus arrives in Manchay, it resembles an exploding tin can with passengers spraying right and left. In the background is a clutch of street merchants cooking great pots of food while another wave of humanity waits to board the bus.

No motorcycles or mechanics in sight.

Chapter 20
Biffies, Houses and Schools

"FAR MORE PEOPLE LACK ACCESS TO A PROPERLY
MANAGED TOILET OR LATRINE THAN WATER."
— World Health Organization

It was New Year's Eve, the last day of 1966, when a string of trucks,
each carrying an outhouse, arrived at a vacant lot and dropped
the structures onto a huge pile. As midnight approached, the
pile was lit, and the sky over Bowsman, a Manitoba village of
three hundred people, glowed from the flames. Cheers rang out
as the village celebrated two events: Canada's centennial year
and the completion of Bowsman's brand new sewage system,
rendering the outhouses obsolete.

On another day, in a later time, it was reported that Portland,
Oregon drained 38 million gallons of water out of the Mount
Tabor reservoir, because a teenager had urinated into it. The
folks in Portland mostly yawned about the water waste. In the
spring of 2014, the village of Westport, Ontario, discharged
partially treated effluent into the Upper Rideau Lake because
its sewage system's lagoon was overburdened. Westport's action
provoked a storm of protest, especially when algae containing
toxins showed up briefly, later in the summer. Don't use or swim

in the lake, don't use the water for cooking or bathing, don't give it to livestock to drink.

Worse was an incident in Walkerton, Ontario, in 2000. Described as the most serious outbreak of E coli ever in Canada, it caused the death of five people, made many others seriously ill, and brought jail time to the water system operators.

Functioning sanitary systems and clean water are deemed basic rights in North America, rights so unalienable that any glitch is news worthy. Not so in third world countries, where clean water is scarce and sanitary systems are far down on the list of priorities for governments and their citizens, even lower than the need for housing. Depending on whose statistics you read, the number of people defecating in the open has either dropped substantially in the first decade of this century, or budged by only a modest figure. Either way, serving the critical need for clean water and sanitation is integral to the HCTH mission and enables the Martins to put workmen they employ on the road to self-sufficiency.

Building outhouses is a practical illustration of how a problem can begat an opportunity, a characteristic of the HCTH approach.

Think about a Ugandan grandfather or a disabled elderly woman, drifting off into the bush as they have all their lives and their dream that, someday within their lifetime, they might just have the luxury, the privacy, and the comfort of an outhouse.

In a country where most of the population lives in rural areas, a latrine is a rarity, a neighbourhood showcase. In fact, newly constructed ones are often featured in the Martins' slide shows.

Sanitary improvements are slow in coming to the slums in all three countries served by the Martins. Clean water is a precious commodity. Hajara and other little African girls in similar circumstances, make daily trips long distances to lug plastic jugs of water back to the household. In fact, fetching water is a constant preoccupation for many in Zambia and Uganda.

In Peru, it is getting water to the homes. Latrines, often as primitive as the homes, are standard, however.

In Africa, a simple outhouse is a major step forward. It is not clear why there is such a dearth of rudimentary sanitary facilities, but then... many things are not clear. It is not a question that crops up in the Martins' conversations; their focus is not on why the situation exists, but what they can to do to fix it.

In Uganda, they visited the site of the new latrine, where HCTH workers were nearly finished digging the hole which was twenty-five feet (eight metres) deep. Hard and hot work at best but with daytime temperatures hovering around thirty plus degrees Celsius, it was brutal by Canadian standards. One fellow digs in the pit and puts the loose ground into a bucket for his partner, who will hoist it to the surface, empty it, and lower it again. Fortunately, the soil is mostly rock free.

It costs about nine dollars a metre for labour. Progress is slow and accompanied by the ever-present risk of a cave-in. Other risks are also present. At another project, the two boys digging the hole hit water at about four metres (twelve feet). Undaunted, they pushed on; everyone concerned recognized the benefits for the neighbourhood.

It takes about three days, on average, to dig the hole, and a week or so to put the structure on it.

Unlike those Manitoba rejects, which were built mostly of scrap lumber, Tom's description of these new latrines suggest they will withstand earthquakes, hurricanes, and torrential rain, handsome additions to their neighbourhood. Solid brick structures with three compartments, two with toilets, and the third for bathing.

HCTH had financed the construction of fourteen latrines by 2015, eight in Zambia and six in Uganda, at a cost of about $800 US each. The demand seems unending.

"Another man asked if we could build him a latrine. He says he just uses the nearby bushes," says one email that could have been sent from any one of a dozen places served by the Martins. An elderly woman had a house built and, with the forty-seven dollars left over from that project, HCTH arranged for workmen to dig a pit for a latrine, and she soon would have her first-ever bathroom. It would be less grandiose, naturally, than the ones just described, but equally well-built and functional.

The value of an outhouse is self-evident, and the Martins were happy to have one to call their own in their early days in Uganda.

Wikipedia reported that in all of Zambia, in 2013, there were thirty-five sanitary water systems. However, only nine were functioning in a country of 6.6 million, leaving half of the population without sanitary facilities. A United Nations study in December, 2014, reported that 25 percent of the basic schools were without safe water and had only limited toilet facilities, one toilet for up to 124 students. The goal is one toilet for twenty-five girls; one for forty boys.

There has been some progress — but apparently in the wrong direction. In 1999, the World Health Organization (WHO) reported that, in Uganda, there was one toilet for 700 students, compared with one for 328 students in 1995. The dramatic statistical change was attributed to more children going to school. It went on to say that only a third of 8,000 schools surveyed had separate boys' and girls' toilets. And in one crisis-affected district, only 2 percent had adequate latrine facilities at all.

WHO then stated the obvious: "In examining the larger issues of waste disposal, we should not forget the role played by the humble latrine. Far more people lack access to a properly managed toilet or latrine than water." The Martins know that and have local tradesmen, who got businesses started with HCTH help, to take on projects when money is available.

In Zambia, Nchimunya is the go-to-guy when the Martins can heed a plea from someone needing an outhouse. Remember Nchimunya? The young entrepreneur who explained to Tom that, "a tool [is] a device that allows to do one's work easier." He is a HCTH success story, a young man who has become a veritable jack of all trades.

Nchimunya started digging pits for latrines and then moved on to more complex endeavours. For example, he built a farrowing pen for the sows at Esperanza, a farm owned by

HCTH, before he started building houses, which now seem to dominate his time.

That's not to say he is out of the toilet business; he built four in 2014. They have to fit in around the demand for houses. In March, 2015, four more families were on his to-do list for houses. These are not split-level, two storey dwellings with plate glass windows and aluminum siding, but solid brick homes with steel roofs and concrete floors. They can be built in a matter of weeks.

Tom reported that "Loveness is very happy to finally have a bathroom. Nchimunya is doing very well." A couple in Ottawa have given him a computer. "He was in shock; he couldn't believe it."

He was unable to try it out immediately though; he was busy plastering a house that HCTH had built the previous year.

Meanwhile, as Nchimunya is building houses and planning others, another Martin protégé has also found his niche. Joel sort of arrived in the Martin world via his daughters, Precious and Esther, who were sponsored by the DeWolfes.

When the Martins and DeWolfes visited the girls' family in the early days of HCTH, the conversations in the tiny house of mud and bricks explored many subjects. The parents were both HIV positive. The mother was very ill; the father, Joel, seemed better, but only worked at odd jobs — when he could find them.

"Joel did piece work, and that might mean something like taking a wheelbarrow from the store to a house. That would be it," said Sterling who, like the Martins, is ever alert to possibilities, and saw a win-win opportunity that dovetailed with several of their projects. Joel was a carpenter, but did not have tools and, as a result, also had no jobs. With tools bought by the Martins and DeWolfes, he began constructing chairs, tables, and beds, and his workmanship made it easy for Tom to sell them, mostly through HCTH, including desks for the school supported by the DeWolfes.

He wrote, in fractured English, to his benefactors, the Martins and DeWolfes, in 2007:

"Thank you for what you have done to my children, Esther and Precious. As you know that me, Joel, am a very poor person. I have nothing to help you Mr. Tom. What can I thank you Mr. and Mrs. Tom. God is the only one who will thank you for all the blessings from the poor children and the poor father and mother."

The Children of the Most High School was among the first beneficiaries of his carpentry talents. In 2007, he started building desks, twenty of them at a cost of $67.10 each, and because Sterling arranged to purchase the necessary angle bars, the cost was far lower than the going commercial rate.

Joel doesn't charge HCTH for his labour, so the Martins give him money at the end of their time in Zambia each year for tools, his house, and other expenses.

The 2007-2008 financial report from the school stated rather wistfully, "If there are any funds left after the window, door, and other jobs are done, we will have to get more desks. We have only 59 desks for our 254 children."

As money came in he added ten more desks in 2014. Emails over the intervening years are dotted with single lines of Joel's assignments, such as these in 2015: "Joel continues to be busy in carpentry. He finished a single bed and now is making a double bed to go into the new house HCTH constructed for Naomi's family, thanks to friends in Guelph, (Ontario). After that, Joel has a small table and two chairs to make for a man named Tom (no relation)."

When Joel finished the beds, Tom used gift certificate money to buy mattresses for them.

One of those mattresses was for Brian, but his greater hope was for his own latrine, so that he could quit using the one next door. The wish popped out as Tom walked with him, listening to Brian's account of his growing-up years.

Brian has had a sad life. Death has been a frequent visitor, beginning with the death of his mother when he was too young to remember. Two siblings had also died as children, and his father died five years ago, leaving him an orphan, who was taken in by an aunt. School wasn't easy, but he prevailed, knowing an education was the only path to his career goal of becoming a lawyer. He failed Grade Nine three times, which meant, in the Ugandan system, repeating Grades Eight and Nine, until he finally succeeded. He was twenty-three.

He got a job in a grocery store, and could have been forgiven for thinking he was now on his way. His aunt, however, had other ideas. Since he was now educated, he had to find his own place to live.

He set up housekeeping in a dilapidated building which had been owned by his father. With his first pay cheque, he bought a door, but the money wouldn't stretch any further. Now, seeing the latrines being built by men supported by the Martins, he dared to dream.

"He was happy with his new bed and mattress," said Tom, adding that Brian, in an unexpected and unusual observation, had expressed thanksgiving that couples such as the Martins spent their retirement years helping others. Tom went on to say that such expressions of gratitude make the stream of appeals for help — the requests always pick up as the Martins' time in the country nears the end — less onerous.

"Yesterday, a lady who HCTH has helped for many years told us she needed a latrine. This morning, the mother of Ruth showed us a house she started to build, but has no money to continue. It is hard to believe that it is only ten a.m."

Chapter 21
The First Convert

"CHRISTIANITY IS A RELIGION OF LOVE."
— Sulah

Although Uganda is identified as predominately a Christian nation, with more than 80 percent of the population aligning themselves with Christian faiths, Muslims are a significant presence — about 12 percent, according to the 2002 census.

Sulah had been one of them. He was the Martins' first convert to Christianity, whose life, and the life of his family, has become part of their own. Tom recounted, in 2013, the email announcement from Sulah and Hajara, his wife, of another child:

Hi Tom good to write to you always and this time am writing to forward you good news, well it wasn't our plan but it came abruptly because we didn't want to have a baby at this time but we found out that Hajara was pregnant by the time our plan was to wait to have a new baby but it came like that. Well we had a new baby 10 December it was Tuesday evening and she was a baby girl and we named her Cheryl because we thought it is a good name. but pray much for our family because at all time we

*experience great things in our life but you are always there for us
as a family...*

On the Martin 2014 scorecard, there were now at least five
Cheryls and five Toms.

The Sulah connection goes back to 2006, in the days when
the Martins were daily visitors to the internet café where his
wife, Hajara, worked. In typical Tom Martin fashion, it didn't
take long for him to befriend any kid who happened to be
around, which inevitably led to conversations with the adults.

As well, Sulah and Hajara's baby, Shamirah, at only a few
months old, offered a bridge between the grandparents who
were away from home and the local couple. Babies do that. No
colour or culture gets in the way of those connections. One day,
Sulah told the Martins that his father had many wives and about
twenty-five children, but cared for none. Eventually, he asked,
"Why do you do business with us?"

Hajara was more to the point. "Why do you love us? We're
Muslim, and you're not."

The answer from the Martins? "It doesn't matter to us; we
have come to help you and your children get a better life." They
explained that they were trying to follow the example of Christ,
by showing love to everyone they encounter.

This couple from Canada certainly seemed different from
the other Mazungus   white folk — who occasionally drifted
through their town. Children are often warned by their parents,
that if they misbehave or don't eat their food, the Mazungus will
come and take them away. Gifts and lots of easy chatter broke
through their wariness. The Martins were the talk of the town,
behind the curtains and likely at the local pub where the men
frequently gathered and kept an eye on these strange Canadians.

Sulah was intrigued. These folks were truly "different." He
wanted to know more.

Tom asked him if he would read the Bible if Tom gave him
one. He agreed, but only if Tom would read the Koran, which
he did.

A couple of weeks later, Sulah sent word that he'd like to "follow Jesus" and proposed a clandestine meeting behind a Red Cross building, away from the prying eyes of neighbours. It was a spot Tom knew well, having previously met the local chairman there to discuss secretly spiriting little Hajara, the house girl introduced at the start of this book, away from her home of bondage.

"I am ready to assure you I am ready to meet Jesus as my savior. Hajara is cool, and me too, and we have decided to follow Jesus."

Sulah sealed his decision with all of its ramifications, switching from Islam to Christ. In a later email to his Canadian supporters, he called Christianity "a religion of love." Almost immediately, he became a regular character in the Martin email saga of activities and events. His footprint is all over HCTH construction projects, ranging from maintenance projects to building new houses, including his own. Most are repairs or improvements.

A sample of his projects is included in Tom notes:

- "I spent much of the afternoon with Sulah, seeing about a water tank for a house.

- We went to see the new door Sulah put on a house for us, [which is] more secure than the old wooden door.

- This evening, Sulah came with the price to put a storage tank and eaves troughs for a family.

- Sulah had to go back on one of his jobs because one of his eaves troughs did not work well. It is better now.

- One of the small buildings purchased by HCTH needs repair work. Tomorrow we are taking [Sulah] to take a look at it.

- Another family needs some work done on their house. The girls want their alcoholic father moved further from their room. They also want a storage area for charcoal and food, so that their father does not steal it to sell."

Like any good friend, especially in Uganda where visits to each other's homes are casual and frequent, Sulah pops in at the Martins whenever the spirit moves him, even when no project is in the immediate offing. Most often, though, there is an agenda. A brother has a family and not much money. He can't pay his son's school fees. Will the Martins pay? The answer is no. He needs to install a concrete floor at his home. Fleas and bedbugs hide in the dust and spraying didn't do the trick. He lacked the cash to pay for the cement and sand. Will the Martins pay? Yes. Could they come to his house? Yes. They stopped in after church on Sunday and were given a basket and mat, both woven by Hajara.

There is a sense that the Martins always need to be alert to requests for aid, and to their own observations of what the household needs. In some cases, it is food; in others, clothing. Each is a judgment call that fits into a bigger juggling act that is influenced by whether the Martins know the petitioner and his or her circumstances. Sometimes a decision can be immediate, but occasionally situations demand more inquiry and detective work before the hard-earned North American funds are dispensed.

It is little wonder the Martins regularly request supporters to pray for wisdom regarding the endless balancing of hand-wringing and requests for help.

"He [Sulah] always wants something," grumped Tom, in an unguarded email.

But such comments are rare and overshadowed by Sulah showing up with three-year-old Gary, a younger brother to Shamirah, wearing new shoes bought for him by HCTH. He likes his shoes. In fact, last night, said his father, he wore them to bed to ensure that he didn't lose them. How do you top a story like that?

In 2015, Sulah wrote to the Canadian family, via the Martins' email, who are sponsors for his daughter, Shamirah. It said, in part:

Our family is happy to have you as part of our family. Every day that passes we are growing spiritually since we were born again. Before we met Tom and Cheryl, we were a young family who had no food to eat, clothing for our daughter, and money to pay rent. Hajara got pregnant while we were in school, but I continued with the help of HCTH and became a mason and builder. God answered our prayers. Tom taught us about change, which was difficult for us, but since we changed to Christianity, we now have love and happiness. We are attracting more people to join Christianity.

His letter describes how he was able to build a home, rather than renting one room, due to the construction work that came his way through HCTH. Hajara has moved on from the internet shop to selling used clothing, shoes, and school bags. They have a garden on the HCTH property and own three chickens. Sulah sounds proud of what his family has accomplished through HCTH, not the least of which is that his children are getting an education. His letters exude the pride of achievement that permeates so many of the communications to the HCTH supporters.

Chapter 22
Farming

"DO NOT WAIT FOR LEADERS; DO IT
ALONE, PERSON TO PERSON."
— Mother Teresa

Karen Blixen's book Out of Africa *opens with what has become an* iconic phrase: "I had a farm in Africa." So does Helping Cope Through Hope — one farm in Zambia and three in Uganda, fulfilling an objective that Cheryl Martin expressed years ago: it was far better to help people help themselves rather than just to give them aid.

A few passersby still stop and gawk at the corn field on the outskirts of Mityana, Uganda, where there's often a white man out there hoeing weeds, an unusual sight. White men generally don't do that here. But that's not all; he is working shoulder-to-shoulder with two Ugandans.

Tom Martin asked the young workers, Barbara and Viola — already knowing the answer —whether this side-by-side field work was common. These were the same two girls who regularly helped the Martins with chores, including gardening at the Martins' home. With a laugh, Barbara responded that local folks don't think white people know how to dig or hoe. She said that

African people think life is so easy in North America that you do not have to work.

They were planting Irish potatoes, two hundred hills of them, before they ran out of seed potatoes. Tom told them that North Americans also have to work, often very hard, as he held open a hole for one of the girls to place the seed potato in the ground. The whole potato is planted, rather than just a section with "eyes" on it, because insects like the quartered potato. Sliced potatoes are like a table set for them. Tom was soaked in perspiration.

A thunderstorm swept through in the evening — "the rain is a real blessing for the gardens that mean life to so many people" — but Tom's crew was back at work the following morning after he and Viola had gone to the market for more potatoes. This large garden is on land purchased by HCTH three years ago, which has been subsequently divided into plots for several families, where they grow an array of grains and vegetables.

When their maize didn't germinate successfully because of poor quality seed, Tom's team was pressed for time, so he made a deal with a woman to replant the field with certified seed. Tom bought her a 50 kg bag of maize flour in payment. She was happy.

When HCTH was founded, the notion of becoming property owners didn't get much of a look-in during discussions about getting kids into school, feeding the starving, and alleviating health problems. Owning land to promote self-sufficiency was a far-off dream, given their limited start-up resources.

But it lurked there, below the surface. So, as funds became available, the Martins bought land for HCTH in both Uganda and Zambia. There are three parcels of HCTH land in Uganda, in the countryside near Mityana, providing a home for two households and livelihood for thirteen families. Two houses are on one parcel that is somewhat larger than one hectare. A bachelor lives in one house, a tiny ten-by-eight-foot building which became larger with an addition built with HCTH dollars. A family of seven lives in the other; they grow vegetables and raise pigs.

"We had been renting a house for them, so having them on the farm made sense," said Tom, adding that the family was becoming somewhat self-reliant, watching a twenty dollar piglet grow as they cared for it. Four other families have garden plots on the same parcel.

No one pays rent on these farms, either in Uganda or Zambia. Tom says, "It's a model no one has tried before, where people get to keep what they grow." People judged by the Martins to be deserving are given use of the land, and they get to keep it, as long as they use it well — and their situation remains the same. Many charity groups have strings and/or costs attached to their land arrangements.

The Martin approach brings reality to the hope embodied in the HCTH philosophy. These are people who, at one point, could not have imagined a life of more than a single meal each day. Imagine — the possibility of breakfast, lunch, and dinner. Every day. And maybe having some produce left over to sell.

One of those who could only dream of a reliable meal every day was Elisha. His family of six was described by Tom as "probably the poorest and saddest" of those helped by the Martins. His eight-year-old daughter had severe brain damage as a result of malaria that went untreated when she was three. Elisha himself hadn't talked until he was fifteen. He sold banana leaves in the market, earning about a dollar a day. HCTH rented land for them to grow crops for a couple of years and sent all the children, except the eight-year-old, to school.

It was the plight of this family that brought Tom up short one day on the rough and tricky motorcycle ride to deliver school supplies to the children. He found himself thinking, "It is easy to get bothered and think that the asking never ends, but then I realize that HCTH is dealing with very poor families. Many children would not even be in school without help. The wonderment more should be how many families would even eat or where they would be if God had not brought HCTH to their door. Elisha is a perfect example."

The Zambian project is entirely different from the farms in the Uganda. Here, the Martins are creating an unplanned, but natural, village, an approach that illustrates the pragmatic and practical ways in which the Martins respond to the vagaries of local circumstances or opportunities.

Historically, villages grew out of societies practicing subsistence agriculture, and were typically small communities with five to thirty families situated together for sociability and defence; the land surrounding the living quarters was farmed. That sums up the HCTH venture in Zambia.

The Martins, in a loose partnership with a Zambian couple, have been building such a village from scratch on a parcel of land near Choma. It isn't clear who, exactly, had the dream as they first walked about the neighbourhood, seeing able-bodied men lounging idly in the shade, as hungry children played in the dust and women tended arid, smoky fires under pots of bubbling maize. But somebody had it.

There was property, a farm actually, being subdivided in the Choma Municipality that prodded the Martins and their friends into action. Quickly, with the blessing of the HCTH board of directors, the three hundred or so supporters in North America became surrogate land owners. About US$3,500 paid for three of the thirty-seven plots in the subdivision, about eight hectares.

They joined forces with Cyrus and Prisca Mfula, described by the Martins as "having the same heart as ours to help the needy in the Choma area. Their problem was a lack of funds, so HCTH decided to partner with them."

The Mfulas are a going concern in their own right. They have organizations which tackle virtually any issue under the rubric of community development, ranging from health to entrepreneurship. Cyrus founded a consultancy to help non-profit and faith-based organizations gain access to funding and to manage their programs. His wife's organization is called Primach Hope Rehabilitation, which targets orphans and vulnerable children while supporting outreach programs.

As native Zambians, their assistance was invaluable in dealing with the local government on land issues. For example, they handled a problem where an adjacent land owner was encroaching on a road allowance. They supervised the re-surveying of the property to end the dispute. They saw it as part of their responsibility, as the managers of the HCTH farm, which is named Esperanza, meaning "hope." The Mfulas have moved from Choma to Lusaka, where they apparently want to replicate Esperanza. Even though the two locations are three to four hours apart, Tom assures supporters that the couple can continue to manage Esperanza. They visit Choma often and are in constant phone contact.

In their 2014 fourth quarter report on Primach Hope Rehabilitation, Prisca Mfula acknowledges the ongoing involvement of HCTH, which has "helped fund most of the programs Primach does i.e. child sponsorship, piggery, gardening, chicken [and] goat [raising] and house building."

The report buzzes with accounts of achievements, improvements made, and families producing almost enough food to provide for their needs.

Pigs and chickens figure large, both in the operation of the farm and off-site farming operations by people helped by HCTH. With minimum instruction, chickens and pigs are relatively easy to raise, and there is a ready market. Getting them to market, however, can be an adventure, such as the day when a bag holding piglets broke, littering the roadway with little porkers. On another day, the conscience of a taxi driver was smitten part way through the trip when he focused on the fact that his cargo included "unclean creatures," to a Muslim. Those pigs and their owner were dumped at the side of the road to await another motorcycle taxi whose driver did not have the same religious conviction.

One December message had a different twist: the Martins reported that ten piglets were born. Then, a few months later: "The pigs are doing well. There are twenty-one ready to sell, but there is a ban on sales because of Swine Fever, but it is to be lifted soon."

The impact of the farming operations extends beyond those directly involved in growing crops or raising livestock. Nchimunya, the young builder shepherded by HCTH, surfaces as the builder-of-record for turning make-shift barns into solid buildings for the piggery and incubators, building fences, and installing irrigation systems.

He built farrowing pens with restraining barriers butting out from the walls, so that sows couldn't roll onto and kill their young. In 2015, the birth of a litter of fifteen piglets was worth reporting, given that fourteen survived the first few days, having been protected by the barriers. They'd be ready for market or breeding in about six months.

Money generated by pig sales provided for feed and porcine medical supplies, crop work, and included a tenth, a tithe, "to bless the families [for Christmas] who have been working tirelessly in taking care of the project."

Nchimunya also built a chicken brooding barn with two incubators paid for by the DeWolfes. The inaugural use was eighty-four eggs to hatch in twenty-seven days. Since the warming lamps offered a fast start for raising chickens, a parallel purchase of four hundred, day-old chicks immediately launched the poultry business. The goal is to expand with flocks of quail, guinea fowl, ducks and turkeys.

Cyrus Mfula had already checked it out. There's always a market for them, and they wouldn't have all their eggs in one basket.

The DeWolfe name is figuratively stamped all over Esperanza, reaching far beyond incubators and chickens. Sterling and Faye were instrumental in underwriting and installing an irrigation system and providing most of the on-going financial support for students and school facilities. They were quiet about the depth of their involvement during my interview with them; it only became apparent from third-party accounts which arrived later. They underwrote most of the sponsorships managed by Primach, which totalled $7,650.

The irrigation system was no small project, involving a submersible pump, an elevated storage tank, and, a network of pipes. The grid of pipes delivering water obviously reduces the anxious looks at the skies during the growing season, as well as the angst reflected in emails. Before the irrigation taps were turned on, we heard that "the planting this year has been delayed a little bit, because there were no signs of rain until about a fortnight ago," even though the ploughing was already done.

Chickens were to be the source of income for Mildred, a widow whose husband died of AIDS, leaving her with three young children. She sold her first flock for meat, requiring the Martins to give a lesson on the cycle of raising chickens. She needed to save some money for feed and buying chicks — about eighty cents each — rather than selling them all.

And then, there's the turn around.

"At five-thirty tonight, someone came to our door with two chickens — cleaned, of course. Yesterday we were given a tray of thirty eggs. Tonight, we are eating omelettes."

To complement his managerial skills, Cyrus Mfula has an entrepreneurial bent. He found that fish farming could be a lucrative business, one that could work at Esperanza. Once the likelihood of success was determined, it was simply a matter of labour to create four fish ponds. The total cost was estimated at $4,800.

A Canadian family paid for the ponds, stocked with a thousand or more bream, a fresh water fish that is described as having a deep, compressed body, silvery scales, and a good taste. Tom idly mused that, "We think we might name the fish pond after them [the donors, not the fish]."

While all this was going on, the Martins were looking for seven goats for a "goat multiplication program." The idea was to give families a male and female goat from which the offspring would then be offered to another family.

"We are very encouraged with the participation of people, especially families living at the farm," said one report. Ninety percent of the businesses that Primach and HCTH helped start were running well. Included in that assessment were loans made to help some individuals get started, and the report said, "Most have paid back their initial loans in full. They can afford to manage the basic things in their homes. And that is success! Those that have paid us back helped us give loans to those who didn't receive [help] the first time."

When the Martins visited in 2015, Tom reported: "This morning, Pastor Sichikata and his wife picked us up at seven a.m. to go to Esperanza. He is building a retirement home there on the farm. He wanted to show us the wire and cement he bought through HCTH support." Six new goats were delivered, as was a new tank and two water taps for the irrigation system.

And finally, the understatement. "There is a lot going on there."

Chapter 23
A Man for all Seasons

"WE COULD NOT FIND A MORE HONEST PERSON."
—Tom Martin

Nothing happens in the Ugandan corner of the Martin world without Joram. From the time he meets them in Kampala to when he bids them farewell at the end of each year's stay, he's there. He lives in the same house, he handles financial matters when they are away, and he crops up regularly in the Martin reports.

So who is he, and how did he come to attain this trusted position with the Martins?

In their earliest days in Uganda, the Martins linked up with a young man named Emanuel who had a basic internet café, which became their link to their Canadian base. As the customer-businessman relationship evolved, Emanuel told them that he planned to become an Anglican priest and had realized that running a business was too much for him during his studies.

But he had an unemployed friend from Kampala named Joram who had some computer training but no money.

Tom explained: "He suggested we should start Joram in computers, which we did. We bought the business for him, which included a generator the Martins had purchased earlier for Emanuel, and got him a couple more computers.

"One of the first advantages of starting a man in the internet business was that there is now a computer in our house."

Turned out, Joram came with the computer. He now has a pseudo-apartment in their home, which also doubles as a guest house when HCTH supporters visit. It works for both: free accommodation for Joram, and protection of their home when the Martins are away. In the process, he has become indispensable as an intermediary and jack-of-all-trades in the Martin universe.

With the Martins only in Uganda for a short time each year, Joram is their designated agent and project overseer in their absence. Given the range of HCTH activities in this country, his role is unique among those who represent the Martins in their absence.

He's thirty-nine, a bachelor in search of a wife. So far, no luck. With few personal distractions, Joram anticipates and undertakes many activities which enable the Martins to achieve far more than they could on their own. Some of the activities are minor, such as picking up Tom at the airport, while others are more complex.

While Tom was delayed one day, Joram had time to take Joan, who is sponsored through HCTH, to university. She had put down a deposit for a hostel room at university, but, as so often happens, they had given the room to someone else. Joram straightened it out before Tom even arrived on the scene.

The benefits of this relationship work both ways. When Mike Shurtliffe and Esther McCutcheon arrived on a working holiday, Mike brought with him his technological expertise and spent much of his time with Joram.

Mike and Esther became Joram's mentors. To help him, they bought items from his shop for others to sell in outlying areas, suggesting that his business had reached beyond computers. Here, as in many countries, if there's a hint of a market, a merchant will try to capitalize on it, even if selling an electrical transformer seems a poor fit with selling shoes.

This entrepreneurial spirit, then, sees Joram now selling toilet plungers along with internet minutes, a sideline born of observing that, when a sink didn't drain properly at the house, Tom bought a plunger. Tom explained how it worked, and it fascinated Joram, He had never seen such a device, but he could see a market for it.

"Joram called at six fifteen p.m. Two sponsored children were at his internet café, saying they need books and a ream of paper for school. Why could they not have come earlier in the day? I told Joram to get the supplies and I would pay him tomorrow."

Look for school supplies to join plungers, internet minutes, and computers in Joram's shop.

Chapter 24
Education

"WHY WAS I EVER CHOSEN TO GO TO SCHOOL?"
— A letter of thanksgiving from Zambia

Change is the only constant in life, even in the work of a mission such as HCTH, which was born with a goal of collecting abandoned children and starting them down the road to an education. There has been an evolution as a result of how deeply entrenched the Martins have become in the lives of the children they sponsor and their families.

When their mission started, the amount of money was very limited, and higher education was beyond the reach of HCTH. More donors now are willing to continue sponsoring a student through university and, as some graduate, a new layer of kids are entering their sphere. Families are big, and often only some of the children have sponsors. As the first wave moves on, younger members of the family can be drawn in, with the older siblings pitching in to help.

Tom leafed through his notes in the spring of 2015 for progress accounts in Zambia, with a focus on higher education, and reported:

- Cathy, the first HCTH university graduate is now working in the United States with plans to further her education.
- Floribert is in his second year of university. He wrote: "Through your love and care, I am making the dream of becoming a teacher a reality."
- Phyllis has one semester of university left before graduating.
- Mutinta is in second year of university. "Someday, I want to lecture at a university."
- Evelyn wrote: "I want to thank you so much for helping me to achieve my dream of attending university. I promise not to let you down."
- Nchimunya is a college graduate now, with a construction business.
- Stedius is in Teacher's College. "It has always been my dream..."
- Patricia is in second year of university.

And there are others:

- Noriah is eleven, in grade six: "Thank you for helping me to go to school and paying for the things I need. I am teaching my mother how to read."
- Farouk does not have a specific sponsor, but needs help with fees to attend school. It was for kids like Farouk that a donor provided enough money for six unsponsored children to attend school.

In their reflective moments, the Martins wonder exactly what doors are being opened by engaged North American donors for bright — some brilliant — young people snatched from the quicksand of poverty. It can be exciting all round when they encounter individuals such as Floribert or Nchimunya who wiggled through every open door in order to achieve a dream. Some doors were mirages, appearing to be an opening but turning into a brick wall, such as a six-month teaching assignment for Floribert without a single pay cheque at the end. Unfortunately, this is not an uncommon occurrence.

"He was amazing. He said it was good experience."

More than 130 kids were being shepherded through schools across the three countries in 2015, with steadily more aided in pursuing higher education.

Could there be another Thokozile Masipa, only the second female black jurist ever appointed in South Africa, lurking in a school uniform in a tiny classroom in the Martins' mission field waiting to be thrust on the world stage? Justice Masipa's beginnings were as austere as many of the HCTH children. The outcome might be less grand, but equally momentous for some young person where hope, wearing a Canadian flag, holds promise.

Justice Masipa illustrates the possibilities. She became known world-wide in 2014 when she presided over the trial of the Blade Runner, the Olympian Oscar Pistorius, charged with the murder of his girlfriend. Mostly lost in the sensationalism of the trial was the remarkable story of Justice Masipa's life which began in a tiny two-room house in Johannesburg's Soweto Township as race violence raged under apartheid, a time when rights of blacks were trampled mercilessly. As a means of suppressing progress, the authorities even forbade them to speak English.

Thirsting to learn, but too poor for university, she worked as a clerk, then a messenger, then an office "tea-girl" and eventually a crime reporter. The rest of her time was divided between raising two children and completing ten years of night school in order to become a lawyer at forty-three. And then a judge.

Giving a child a chance has been the fundamental *raison d'etre* of Helping Cope Through Hope since the outset. Several hundred young people in three countries make up the Martin alumni, filling HCTH scrapbooks with stories of successes, near-successes, and fortunately, only a few downright failures. But it's a mission without end. Jimmy, Esther, Manuel, Annet — the list is long and getting longer. None drops off the "family chart." The Martins don't let go of their charges part way through their education — as long as they are diligent. As the organization matures, education is still its most dominant aspect, even if poverty and social issues now compete, and sometimes overshadow it.

In 2014, their "children and grandchildren" included several university students in Zambia and Uganda. It is a gratifying accomplishment, but coming with the satisfaction is the financial implication. Fees and associated costs amount to about $2,000 a year per student, and may go higher, with tertiary costs such as the need for computers, class supplies and clothes.

So it was a triumph when a 2015 email began, "Jimmy called us last night to say he had some good news for us."

A few years back, Jimmy had showed up with accounts of how he only ate once a day to save money to pursue his education with HCTH assistance, chasing his dream to work in broadcasting. Now, he had a job with a radio station, reporting sports stories and doing play-by-play announcing. Among his assignments was reporting a Premier League soccer game against England, no small achievement.

The Martins see a growing number of young "Jimmys" seizing opportunities provided by HCTH. Perhaps not as dramatic as Justice Masipa, or on as big a stage as broadcasting, but still rewarding, both for them and for the Martin network.

In Uganda, in 2015, seventy-five children were in school and fifteen others were in university, thanks to HCTH supporters. Agnes is among the university students. She was the first child the Martins sponsored in Uganda. She completed one year of college, then worked as a waitress in Dubai for two years, before returning home with a desire to complete her education. Now studying journalism, she is also the owner of a photo studio, using equipment bought for her by Mike and Esther, who spent two weeks in Mityana in 2014. The couple had donations from others as well as their own cash. Mike was the young man who cautioned another potential supporter, saying, "If you go, don't take your credit or bank cards — you'll max them out. There is so much need."

The caution was supported as Tom wrote about Mike and Esther's activities: "Yesterday ... they purchased a nice video camera for Agnes for her college journalism course. They purchased a new printer for Joram's internet shop, and a textbook for Barbara in Grade Thirteen."

While Mike was working side-by-side with Joram, Esther met, worked and played with children, including two who shared her name. But it was Hope Angela who caught Esther's interest. It is always fascinating to speculate what's hit a "hot button" that changes an encounter into a connection. Hope Angela had been turfed from school because she hadn't paid the forty dollar fee. The Canadians picked up the cost, and Tom wrote that, "If Hope Angela's father had problems paying for term one, there is a good chance it would be the same for terms two and three. [They] wanted to pay [those fees as well.]"

In the same email, Tom remembered that he had gone to Hope Angela's father, Michael, to get his bicycle repaired. "He fixed it for no charge."

That minor repair shot Tom off on another tangent, the saga of a sister and brother he and Cheryl were trying to stick handle through the administrative roadblocks to get them re-enrolled in school, a long and frustrating process they experienced over and over again.

Both kids were ready for Grade Twelve. Maria missed Grade Twelve the previous year, because she was unable to pay the associated fees. Now, with HCTH help, both Maria and Julius were ready to move on. Not so fast: Tom instructed them to bring their Grade Eleven results, and he would accompany them to register for Grade Twelve, but Julius could not get his marks, since he had not paid last year's fees. The bill was about one hundred dollars, and Tom was hopeful that, with the payment, both students would be good to go.

And here comes the connection with Michael: "They will have about a forty-minute walk to school, so God put it on our hearts to give them our bicycles. That is why I was getting them in good repair."

For Tom, the first day of any school term brings the greatest frustration. Uganda provides, supposedly, Universal Primary Education (UPE) which is free to Grade Seven. One year, Tom wrote: "Today, Hassan and Shafic could not go to school because they did not have an inside broom, an outside broom, and four rolls of toilet paper to take to school," even though their fees had been covered by HCTH. Another school's list was more extensive: eight rolls of toilet paper, two four-litre cans of paint and a scrub brush, while a high school required laundry soap and a slasher, a tool known elsewhere as a machete.

A headmaster explained that the two kilograms of sugar he required each term was for the porridge which was served to the students each morning, but Tom believed the bags were going to find their way to the teachers.

Tom complained that Kate could not go to school for the same reason — no broom, no toilet paper, etc. And Rebecca, in Grade Nine at Mityana Secondary School, was sent home because she did not have a ream of duplicating paper, which each student must bring each term.

"If each student in a school of a thousand students brings four rolls of toilet paper, that means four thousand rolls are taken in by the school. Also, they get a thousand inside brooms and a thousand outside brooms. Some schools demand a long handled brush, so they have a thousand of them and a thousand reams of photocopying paper, too.

"Each ream has five hundred sheets. Most people know that the schools sell some of these items, which they do not need. Sadly, many children are not going to school, because they can't afford these items."

Tom shifted gears: "I took two other children to the market to get school supplies. One of them is leaving today for boarding school. Boarding is expensive, because the students need lots of other items, such as soap to bathe and wash clothes with, a bucket for water, a basin for bathing, a towel, sheets, mattress, pillow and much more."

Despite the frustrations, or perhaps because of them, Tom writes about the upside — being able to tell a parent that someone in Canada wants to help their child through sponsorship.

There is also an undercurrent of satisfaction when, at day's end, he reflects on the first day of a school term: "We left home this morning at eight thirty a.m. and returned about five p.m. We paid school fees for thirty-four children from eleven different schools. Two of these were for university..."

Many sponsored children live in boarding schools, due primarily to the distance from home to school, but it goes against the grain for Tom, the former teacher. Some children are as young as three. He recounts what some students told him about their schedule. Up at three a.m., classes of some sort from four to six thirty, and then regular classes from seven thirty to six p.m., with an hour off for lunch, which is "posho and beans." Dinner is six forty-five p.m., with more posho and beans and night classes to nine thirty. Posho is corn flour cooked with water, a kind of porridge.

"I know many of you don't believe, me but sadly, it is true. Where are the studies that show teenagers need more sleep?"

Despite their misgivings, the Martins put Barbara into a boarding school after they found her a sponsor. It was there that their role as surrogate parents for this young orphan was cemented. They approved her absences from classes, arranged medical appointments, and bought her clothes and school supplies.

Throughout the years of email messages, Barbara continued to be a presence, which reinforces the impression that she holds a special spot in the Martin universe. It was Barbara who introduced the Martins to Annet, the young mother with AIDS. She also introduced them to the national sport of netball, and was also a frequent companion for work and leisure.

Tom holds a prejudice against boarding schools due to the treatment of students, but his criticism is more general when he focuses on language.

"No one graduates from Grade Seven; the teaching is so poor," he says. English is taught in the schools, but the quality can be shaky. "The head teacher's room had some interesting reading. One sign said, 'How to help slow *leaners*.' I think they meant learners. Another said, 'Our school *Moto*.' Another said, 'you need a school badge — *Orang* in colour.'"

A road sign encouraged readers to "Get your *eyez* checked *hear*."

State-administered schools in Zambia and Uganda are concerned primarily with the lower grades. Starved for financing, quality suffers in all the schools.

The current education system in Uganda is only about fifty years old, but the state attendance law is often trumped by the reality of families having to choose between food and education. Similarly, in Zambia, education, particularly in rural areas, is spotty. Facilities, supplies and quality instruction are mostly absent, a reflection of the subsistence economy.

In both Uganda and Zambia, education is closely aligned with religion with most of the major schools run by church organizations. An early Martin report mentioned taking school supplies —books, stapler, scissors, flashcards, and an electronic A-B-C board — to St. Anne School, which was operated by the Roman Catholic Church with an Anglican head master.

"It is great how people work together," Tom said, adding, "It was good to see a pile of Gideon New Testaments on his desk, ready to give to each of the five hundred students."

In Peru, the educational environment is not quite so bleak, although poverty feeds miserable school achievements there as well. Battling its effects provides a field of opportunity for HCTH, even though, officially, Peru boasts a literacy rate of more than 90 percent.

Here, the dynamics stand in sharp contrast with Africa. In Peru, the Martins' effort to keep children in school is more about helping the families that are unable to pay for uniforms and supplies rather than the questionable demands for materials ranging from brooms to toilet paper. There are also more distractions for the vulnerable — the lure of video shops, if a few coins can be scrounged.

Tom shakes his head in despair in recounting the example of a sponsored youngster in Peru, who threw it all away to hang out at a video shop in hopes that someone would stand him to an occasional game. He is even more despairing, however, when he and Cheryl discuss the epidemic of teenage pregnancy. It is a world-wide issue, but is most prevalent in third world countries. The United Nations estimates that the deaths of 6.3 million children and 289,000 women a year are preventable. Women who give birth before the age of fifteen are five times more likely to die during child birth, with attendant risk to the infants.

The Martins confront the early pregnancy reality every day in their mission fields. Young girls get caught in the trap of unwanted parenthood and perpetual poverty — if they even survive. A surgeon in Mityana said that many girls, especially in rural areas, are pregnant by Grade Seven, and then have to leave school. He did not mention mortality rates.

The Martins strive to break the cycle for the young mothers, with the goal of getting them back into the classroom. Their intervention begins with providing food, clothing, accommodation, and often child care.

Successful interventions — and there are many — provide the continuing incentive for Tom and Cheryl to keep trying, even when there are setbacks or failures.

Chapter 25
Cynthia

"WE CAME TO LOVE HER VERY MUCH."
— Tom Martin

Whenever the Zambian kids gathered around the Martins to sing, play games, or hear Bible stories, there was a girl of eleven, maybe twelve, in the shadows. Her wistful eyes followed the activities. She'd crane her neck to watch as the others wrote and drew cards with Cheryl. She'd smile as Tom told Bible stories and made the children laugh with funny stories. But she didn't join, in and that's the kind of kid who draws in the Martins.

Cynthia was her name. She had epilepsy.

The Martins began watching her reactions as the group learned church choruses, heard stories, played games, and drew pictures which they could take home. Obviously she was itching to participate but was too timid or intimidated to join in. As they showed their interest in her, particularly Cheryl, her guard gradually slipped, and she slowly began to lose her sense of being an outcast.

"She'd come over while others were in school, and we'd encourage her by teaching her how to write her name," Cheryl said. She was careful not to pry, but learned, bit by bit, about what had been shaping Cynthia's lonely childhood. She had siblings, including a twin. Her father had AIDS and was ill. Her mother paid her scant attention, partly because of her affliction, and also because, as the one working parent, Cynthia's mother was focused on earning her meagre income by making and selling beer. Cynthia simply drifted, alone and lonely.

"Why aren't you in school?"

"I can't."

"Why not?"

"Nobody to pay. I can't read."

When the other kids were in school, Cynthia made personal connections with paper, pencils, and books, all those items she had longed for from a distance. Painstakingly, following Cheryl's finger across the page, she learned the letters of the alphabet and then how to string them together.

"We came to love her very much," Tom said. "We paid for her to go to school for the first time in her life, we had clothes made for her, and bought others, we provided her with nutritious food, and epilepsy medication. We spent a lot of time loving her. We enrolled her in school in March. On April 8, it was a Saturday morning, her sister, who we also helped by buying some clothes and a blanket, banged on the door."

Their father had died. The Martins helped with funeral arrangements and expenses.

"We grieved with the family. We went to the home; we walked one and a half hours to the grave site."

Then, the unthinkable happened. This time, it was an early morning telephone call. Cynthia had died. Once again, the Martins went to the home to join the family. There was much wailing and shrieking, which struck Tom as unusual, given how Cynthia had been abandoned for so long. They were "wailing as if they cared," he said.

Her body was laid on the floor, because there was no money to pay for transporting her to the mortuary. The Martins paid. The family planned to bury her in a sack, but the church wanted a proper funeral. The Martins paid.

His voice caught in the telling:

"She was our special little friend, and we know we will see her again someday. The fact that we were there for the last five weeks of her life was the greatest experience of my life. To pay for her funeral, to have paid for the dress out of material from Canada that she was buried in … to see her wrapped in the blanket we bought for her, to be able to put a wreath of grass on her grave, to be part of making a cross from beads given us in a bracelet by a lady in Napanee. It was an awesome experience."

Cynthia's death left a hole in the Martins' life, which left them vulnerable on another day.

It had been a long one, filled with distributing money and collecting donor letters, when a woman with a teen-aged boy arrived at their gate. He couldn't see well, she explained, and needed eighty dollars for eye surgery. Maybe it was the time of day, the weariness of constant interaction with people needing help, or the rawness of Cynthia's death, whatever, the Martins gave the money.

Next morning, the boy was at the gate with a new twist to an old tale. The woman, whom he had identified the night before as his mother, had run off with the money and left him stranded. He still needed surgery. Could they help? Once bitten, twice shy.

The local pastor suggested that the "mother" and boy may have seen the Martins on the street and, because they were white and by extension wealthy, had followed them home.

"It was the only time we gave money to someone we did not know. The only time."

Normally, they refer strangers to a local church, which has a benevolent fund. "We can't help everybody. We do research, get to know the family." Except for that once. "We never help someone at the gate if we don't know the situation."

Sifting through the merits of each request, they make decisions leavened by compassion and guided by experience. Rare mistakes occur and are more than balanced by the love and care they provide to those in need, like Cynthia, the lost soul who blossomed with their caring and whose memory is ever with them. They hesitate, weighing the impact of whatever decision is made, and think of her.

"We were shelling peanuts. It was raining hard. There was a knock on the gate and there was a lady there with a very handicapped child. The child was severely handicapped — the mother had to support its head. The help that child needed was far beyond what we could do.

"We felt really bad, but we had to send her away. We couldn't help. Nobody could help." Tom is silent, perhaps weighing again whether there would have been something they could have done, like the way they had done with Kenny. He was a little boy with cerebral palsy who, when they had met, was lying on the mud floor in a poor shelter. The Martins got him enrolled in a school for handicapped children, and witnessed his joy when they delivered a new wheelchair bought with HCTH dollars, one designed for a child.

There is little time, however, for second guessing. Someone seeks funds for AIDS medication, the neighbours come, kids need school supplies, a brother or cousin or neighbour needs food — twenty to thirty requests a week.

Still, it is the balancing of requests against the availability of money and need that weighs on them. Cheryl says she finds it easier to say no than Tom, who, she claims, is more responsive. He talks of dysfunctional families with absentee fathers and wayward children, of hard-luck stories that can rip his heart. One family where the mother was run over and killed by a car; another with a mother who is pleading because her children would be denied school attendance for unpaid fees. Mixed into the real needs are the out-and-out transparent scams, such as the boy who claimed he needed a bicycle to go to school, which, it turned out, was just blocks away.

Periodically, Tom's journal entries and emails aren't so much reports as ruminations, reflecting the depth of compassion as he struggles with the constant flow of need: the persistent boy who came to ask for help to finish his last year in high school. But Cheryl was alone when he arrived, and asked that he return when Tom would be back. Four times he returned, until he caught them both.

"He is from a very poor family. He said last year his mother dug in a garden for someone to get school fees. This year, fees are more, because he has to pay to write National exams. This fee is about $55. The total he needs is about $120. Can we help just one more?"

But it is never just one more. A young woman they knew had to stop taking a knitting course because her aunt, who had been helping her financially, couldn't help any more. She had rent to pay and was expecting a baby in August. The Martins took her to a lady who taught on the knitting machine, and who said if she was good, she might hire her. Could they help in the interval?

These are the decisions they face every day.

Amongst the litany of misery, there are rays of sunshine. Stories of successful completion of training, good marks achieved, or a job or a business started. Those are the stories that refresh the spirit, such as the often-repeated story of three-year-old Gary, who wore his first-ever pair of shoes to bed.

Chapter 26
The Girls of Uganda

"THIS ONE LIFE ALONE MAKES WHAT GOD
DOES THROUGH US WORTHWHILE."
— Tom Martin

In many places, AIDS is still a death sentence. Despite impressive medical progress, it continues in epidemic proportions in some countries where the diagnosis can presage unrelenting misery, wasting away over weeks, months, or occasionally years, before death arrives as a release from it all. Annet knew the cycle, and her heartache was compounded by Kate, her baby girl whom she had farmed out to a neighbour, "so that she wouldn't see her mother die."

When she was fourteen or fifteen, Annet had been a house girl at the home of a bishop. There was also a boy. He abandoned her after making her pregnant, leaving her with a baby and AIDS.

When the Martins first met Annet, she was a skeleton, her body wracked by the disease, without even the most rudimentary medical support, because she was destitute. Barbara, one of the children the Martins sponsored, was her friend. They gathered firewood and fetched water together, but Annet's waning health cast a heavy cloud over the typical teen-age girl chatter.

Could the Martins help? They demurred initially — money, as always, was short — but then they met her. Annet was very, very sick. Not much more than skin and bones. Tom touched her arm, which felt like a bone with no flesh. She could barely walk; her joints were swollen and painful.

She had tried to get help at the AIDS clinic, but it was overwhelmed with 4,000 patients coming from a town of 5,000 and its large catchment area. Lines were long, but even when she was strong enough to wait, the staff was out of medicine by the time it was her turn; people with money got treated first. Tom wrote: "First thing we did was get Annet a big bag of food she needed. We gave her money so that she could go to hospital and start on medication. It was thirty-two dollars for three IV drips and other medication, money provided through HCTH gift certificates. The medication would at least prolong her life. We had a chance to pray with her.

"A young Canadian couple, [Mike and Esther] came with money from their family, and what they did for Annet is unbelievable."

Tom quoted Esther's father as saying that he had, over the years, given a lot of money to charity but had never seen it at work. This time he did. Money was left for food, medicine and transportation to and from the hospital. Meanwhile, Tom had looked at Kate's last report card (part of Grade Two) before she had had to drop out, and he took her to meet the principal. Since she had been first in her class, Tom asked if she could go into Grade Three. The principal agreed. It was a scene repeated again and again, her top-grade marks allowing her to move through primary school quickly. She continued to excel with each new challenge. Kate is a "really smart little girl" who'll "never have to worry [about being able to go to school] again."

As for her mother, Annet brims with new-found confidence fed by good food and life-prolonging medication, and is ready for whatever life brings her. Re-born, in a physical sense; born again, in a spiritual sense.

Annet is "a different person — the change is unbelievable," Tom said, and paraphrased comments she herself had made on the changes in her life.

"Before taking ARVs, my life was miserable, with no hope. I felt I was all alone. After meeting Tom and Cheryl, they helped me out. Then, I met Mike and Esther. These people gave me hope and courage that I would be fine. Now I am fat. I have a nice smile. I think I am looking good. Am I? My body and breasts are not shrivelled up any more. Kate is healthier too. I want to tell Esther's Dad and Mom that I will always be praying for them."

Tom's personal footnote reads, "This one life alone makes what God does through us worthwhile."

Aside from all the support given to Annet to fight her disease, HCTH paid for some computer courses, and, when her first job (twenty-five dollars a month) left her with no money after paying to get to and from work, the Martins intervened to have Joram hire her in his computer shop. The ultimate goal, however, is for Annet to receive a university education, and these jobs are intermediate steps.

Her Canadian sponsors are committed to underwriting Annet's university studies, assuming her marks hold up.

Annet's appearance in the Martins' life, at a time when she was at rock-bottom with no hope for any kind of future, emphasizes Tom's frequent observation that, "God just puts people in our path." It is a crooked path, leading up and down the dusty streets, into schools and hospitals. But, he says, with a hint of awe in his voice, "we give thanks that we can help."

Annet's friend Barbara was a youngster whom God put in the Martins' path earlier. She came from what, by North American standards, would be described as a dysfunctional family. Her mother, a prostitute, died when Barbara was seven, and her sister, Viola, was five. Her father, a witch doctor, had six wives. When his HIV became full-blown AIDS, wife number six sent him back to number one, because she wasn't "paying for no funeral."

Barbara was attending an orphan school, a public school where standards are minimal. The Martins moved her to a boarding school, a better option, even though Tom is critical of those institutions.

Barbara had been ill. She said she had typhoid, as did about half of the 160 girls in her dorm at boarding school. Some of the girls slept two to a bed. They often drank unboiled water. As she recovered, they received a telephone call from her; she needed permission to leave school to get a haircut, get her school uniform sewn, and buy jerry cans and flip flops.

"Since we are really her parents, we had to arrange this for her. We took the opportunity to have lunch with her, then take her to visit her friend Annet, then to her home to see her sisters for the first time in two weeks, and to see her niece, Joceline, who calls her mommy."

Barbara told them about her step brother's graduation party. She and Viola cried when the master of ceremonies centred out their father, Joseph. The speaker said, "This is the father who never paid for any of his sons' schooling…" The girls said they knew their father was an alcoholic, but they loved him, and wept at the cruelty.

After the Martins first met and decided to help the girls, the aid extended to the whole family: buying mattresses, building a house to replace their hovel, underwriting school fees, buying books, school supplies, and clothes. In the process, it seems that Barbara stuck to them like glue, full of chatter, helpful, and enthusiastic; her talk was endless and often swirled around her love of netball.

Finally, curiosity prevailed. "What IS netball?" Well, it is a variation of basketball with seven players with assigned positions on each team. Women and girls are the most likely participants in a sport that is played by about 20 million worldwide. It is huge in Africa, especially in school. Barbara told them she was a good player. Given that the Martins arrange their Christmas break to coincide with the hockey schedule of their grandson, it was a foregone conclusion that they were interested in watching her play. They discovered that she was, indeed, a very good player.

It was the final district game and the Martins were in the stands, proud as any parent. "It was kind of emotional for us. She was named the most valuable player in the league."

As the elimination rounds continued and the competition kept getting tougher, Barbara said she needed a particular kind of running shoe. The Martins bought the shoes. Barbara was voted the most talented netball player in Uganda in 2014, a status that would help her in her quest for bursaries and scholarships.

Her sister, Viola, was also an excellent player, whose team had come second in their district on their way to the national playoffs. She had been given a bursary to help cover the cost of living at a boarding school, with the balance paid by HCTH. In 2015, she was one of a handful of students whose transition from secondary school to college was being guided — and financially supported — by the Martins. Tom did not say whether he had budgeted for a special pair of running shoes.

Naturally, the Martins focus on the successes. They don't dwell on the failures, partly because of the hurt and disappointments that surround them. But of course there some.

One morning began with a visit to the home of a student who had been sponsored for some time. She had blamed Joram, the Martins' agent in Uganda, for many of her ills, including her poor school performance.

"This was the last straw for us and we told her that HCTH would not sponsor her any more. The family has a history of being difficult to deal with. This is one of the times when the decision felt right after it was done. Things are not always [that] easy."

Some names, such as Barbara and Annet, come up regularly in Tom's emails. Others appear once or twice and then slip into the shadows, only to appear a week or month later as though they'd never been missing. It is a continuum; children grow up, students graduate, families change, more or less outside the scope of involvement by the Martins. At the same time, others are drawn into the Martins' net. There are now several Cheryls, pronounced in a variety of ways, and a few Toms.

"Today, within an hour, I met both a Tom and a Cheryl," wrote Tom, reporting on a visit to the market. Imagine the mix a few years hence.

While the make-up of their constituency changes with time, The Martins stay in touch with many, including Agnes, the first child they sponsored in Uganda, and her friend Ritah, the first of her extended family to complete high school.

Tom went to Kampala to catch up with Ritah, who now is married to a pastor and has a child. She and her husband have a group of thirty-five children whom she works with in Katwe, the largest slum in Kampala. With a tarp for a roof over them and wooden benches beneath them, "the children love God and they love to sing … Ritah led them in an hour long program of music, dance, and acting." He reported that when he left, more than thirty of the children accompanied him on the fifteen-minute walk to the taxi stop.

The following is one of Ritah's emails to the Martins, in which she brings them up to date on her life after meeting them:

[I] am so happy to hear from u too, it always blesses my heart. Yes I have a baby boy he is two and a half years. [I] am married to a pastor [and] we are having a church in Kampala. We built seven rooms for the people who do not have anywhere to live and for the young children under our care.

Yes am working. I have a hardware shop and my husband also works hard to carry on the big dream of helping others. Our church is called the shepherd's house (a home of Temple Warriors). Some come with just an intention of getting a place where to sleep but with time they decide to give their life to Christ.

So we welcome all people from all religions. We don't force them to give their lives to Christ but we show them that Christ is the best with [our] actions. Every Sunday we leave food for them which will take them through the week. Most of them don't have jobs and others are old. Others come when they are chased by their parents because they are pregnant. We have had so far four girls and now their children have grown up and we have shown them that our God gives a second chance now.

On Sunday we are launching what we called food box for the Temple Warriors. We want them at least not to lack food that is the basic need. I love you friends and may the lord bless you. Ritah

Ritah's friend, Agnes is also one of the Martins' poster students. Their first brush with her was by happenstance, or divine intervention, an encounter while walking through the compound where she lived. She said later that she and Ritah had fasted and prayed for three days that somehow they would be able to go to school. She was certain Tom and Cheryl arrived in her yard as an answer to those prayers. It was the start of a lasting relationship.

The challenges for the Martins are constant, with more than one hundred kids just a key stroke away, and Agnes, in the emails over four months, touches on them all. She begins with thanking the Martins and God, and then casually mentions that the distance from home to school is "very far" and "costly for transport every day." Then, she praises God for the "miracle of school fees" but needs prayer because "[I] am footing to reach school because I do not have money for transport to school." She reiterated that she lives far from school.

Tom replied sternly that he had arranged for her to receive money for travelling to school during her last term. "Please do not ask for any more. We cannot give you more than this. We are praying you do well in your last term."

They saw her through Grade Thirteen, stayed close while she worked for two years in Dubai and, at the age of twenty-five, was one year away from completing college. Her course of study was journalism, and her Canadian sponsors gave her, in addition to other items, a camera, to be used in the pursuit of her career. It was the springboard to a photo studio which she now owns.

Chapter 27
Praying and Dreaming

"WHEN FACED WITH UNCERTAINTIES,
THINK OF THEM AS POSSIBILITIES."

—Unknown

The Martins bought a house in Mityana in 2015, a place where children, mostly orphans, could live safely and go to school. Tom's emails traced every step in the process, from checking availability to cutting the grass. One Canadian in particular tracked every step from afar, because he's the one who made it happen.

It all began with a casual conversation with a man — who wishes to remain anonymous — in which Tom described the problems of many youngsters whose education was impeded by poverty. This individual was already heavily engaged in the Martins' work, having sponsored university students. Tom talked about the particular difficulty faced by children who lived too far from schools, particularly secondary schools. As well, there were the kids abandoned to the streets who had a perilous existence.

Those abandoned kids should be in school. If only HCTH could afford a place for them to live, they could be sponsored.

The man was intrigued: "How much would a house cost?"

"Less than you'd think. Maybe $20,000."

"Find it and I'll buy it. But, wait a minute. Who'd look after those kids if they lived there?"

"We'd have to find a house mother or house parent."

"Find someone and I'll pay."

"Wow."

Such generosity, such passion — where did it come from? Tom wondered. The businessman's personal story unfolded as the link between them grew stronger. This man understood poverty. As a young man, between jobs, broke and couch surfing, his future seemed bleak, when a friend, whose couch was the man's temporary home, steered him toward a salesman's job with an insurance company. He was good at it and, with the passage of time, became the owner of his own business.

He eventually sold it, and, with no dependents, was using the money to honour the God who had blessed him, by helping people less fortunate. Those in Uganda and Zambia fit his criteria.

The smell of money for someone who was ready to part with a house wafted through the town. Mityana doesn't have a real estate board with a multi-listing system, but the hint that a buyer might be around certainly generated gossip and flushed out sellers. Sulah's father had a building for sale. Joram's friend Boaz had two available. The Martins were not looking for a house with island kitchens, multiple bathrooms, finished basements — all the selling features for a house in Canada. They were looking for a place with sturdy walls, waterproof roof, and several rooms for beds — these essentials served to eliminate many of the offerings.

Tom's conversations with this man have already been featured in another chapter. He was the businessman who asked about the annual cost for two university students. When he was told it was about $1,800 a year each, he agreed to pay it, and soon after, to pay $1,200 to save one of his sponsored student's father from losing his house.

Eventually, the Martins found their dream home: a three-year-old duplex — "boys will stay on one side, and girls on the other." Negotiations dragged on for months. After climbing over many hurdles, higher and more complicated than one would face in North America, the house became theirs. Earlier land purchases by HCTH prepared them for the twisted path to ownership, and now an occupancy date was set.

In anticipation, they spent two days in the market buying sheets, pillows, charcoal stoves, pots, dishes, and utensils. Then, they hit a snag; one of the tenants hadn't left, and it was already 4:30 p.m. on the day the Martins were to take possession.

They were at the gate with new bunk beds, mattresses, and bed linens, anxious to see the back of the departing tenant on the closing date. They watched and waited all evening and then gave up until the following day, when they took up the wait again. Finally, at about 10 p.m., the tenant left.

Of course, the tenant took the bulbs from the sockets. That's also normal, just like the late night move. That's when many Ugandans move, it seems, so that neighbours do not see what they have and what they've taken. It was expected that whatever wasn't nailed down was likely to have left with the tenant. What they did not expect, however, were the holes in the walls, evidence of the disappearance of the wooden moldings.

The following morning, the Martins and three girls, who were not in school that day, scrubbed the walls and outside porches. The reward for the girls was being taken for lunch, small pancakes and soda.

Cheryl and Barbara, the net ball player, the Martins' shadow, worked inside, while Tom began the task of cleaning the yard. Barbara stayed for dinner — potatoes, beans, and two muffins that Cheryl had made "a week ago," which they had with milk. The milk was a first for Barbara, and then Tom brought out the Jell-O, another first. Tom had told her, "You always have room for Jell-O."

"Tomorrow, Barbara will help Cheryl wash clothes. I think I mentioned before that, in Uganda, it is all done the way it was done in North America before the invention of the washing machine."

There wasn't even an old fashioned wash board to make rubbing out stains and grime easier, just determination, strong hands and a strong back.

Tom, meanwhile, drove all the way to Kampala to buy cement to fix the gate, and razor wire for the wall around the property.

By mid-May, 2015, nine young people, plus a house mother, would be living there.

Among them was Miriam who caught up with the Martins to ask if she could stay in the house over the Easter break, rather than return to her uncle's home for the holiday period. Just before moving in, she had to miss school to care for the uncle's children while he visited the village. She had a history of being caned, often without reason, and at least on one occasion because she gave left-over food to a friend rather than throw it out.

"She had all her belongings in a backpack ... her skirt was a little frayed ... I asked her if she had many clothes ... she said no ... looks like another trip to the market."

The house was clean, the pantry was loaded, and Annet was in charge. Gradually, a routine evolved, and "the girls said [that in] the last few weeks, they have eaten the best they ever have in their lives," a comment that caused Tom to reflect on eating habits, In Uganda, when there is abundance, they eat until they are uncomfortably stuffed, not sure when or where the next meal will come from.

"We talked to Annet about that tonight when we bought peanut flour to go with their matooke [a dish made from green bananas]. We felt there was enough for two meals but unless told otherwise, they would use it for one, eat very large portions and throw out what is left."

The Martins also wanted to instill the concept of menu planning to include a variety of foodstuffs such as tomatoes, cabbage, and peanut sauce to accompany the posho, matooke, or rice. They scheduled a meeting with the girls living in the house, setting rules for turning out lights, conserving water, and eating balanced and healthy meals. Planning has to be taught, in keeping with the Martins' determination to be "wise with the money [and food] God blesses us with," which, on one specific day, included a chicken.

It could have been a mixed blessing without the versatile Barbara. The Martins had been given chickens for distribution to needy families. Two were for them, one for the Martins themselves, and one for the HCTH house. The problem was that they were alive, and even though Tom had been raised on a farm with many chickens, dealing with blood and guts weren't in his job description. Barbara had no such reservations, stepping in to kill and dress them.

Barbara also teamed up with her friend Annet to cook a meal for the children who would be living at the new house. Tom described it:

"We decided to eat in the new house ... The lunch time was set for twelve. Barbara and Annet came with the food at one fifteen ... it was an excellent meal ... beef, pork, spaghetti, potatoes, peanut sauce, and rice." Sodas and donuts finished it off. Eating with the children involves lots of laughter, and that meal was no exception, with Faridah [one of the new residents] being the focus. Now a Christian and attending a school affiliated with the Anglican Church, she was introduced to pork, a meat forbidden to her as a Muslim — "she came back for seconds."

The wait for dinner to arrive gave Tom time to make yet another trip to the store, to buy moldings, and then to help Cheryl put up mosquito netting and a clothes line. On one of the trips, he took Barbara with him to buy a rack on which to dry dishes. She didn't quite understand what Tom wanted to buy, and got him the price on a brand new coffin instead. Amid hoots of laughter and linguistic gymnastics, they got it straightened out.

Acquiring other necessities was less fraught, although equipping and organizing the new house for a dozen or so occupants is an exhausting and demanding task. Then Prossy contracted malaria, a disease that can cause horrific damage if left untreated. It can hit again and again, almost as often as a common cold in Canada. In close quarters, it leapfrogs from one to another.

Under Cheryl's watchful eye, Prossy quickly recovered, but there was no cure for her saddened heart; when Cheryl asked how her mother was, Prossy broke into tears and reported her mother was ill. In Uganda, that means AIDS. Despite her sadness, Prossy took stock of her good fortune in her new surroundings by writing to her benefactors:

I thank you for whatever you have done for me and my family. One of the days which made me and my heart happy was the day you brought me into this big, nice, lovely, beautiful, handsome new house. First of all it has been my first time to sleep in a house with a gate. I was getting everything that I needed. The first was the care. I thank you all because you have taken care of me since I came into this house. Second of all is feeding. Since I came into this house I started feeding on a balanced diet … because here in this new house we are eating cabbages, rice, vegetables, posho, beans and drinks like soda and milk and water and so many others.

I thank Almighty God that has given you life and money to buy this house. May God reward all who combined to work and pray to buy this nice looking house. In our home place we could not get better care than the care you give us.

Although parents have parental care but there is a care that Cheryl provides to you which is better than your mother, that when you are sick, she asks how you are feeling and then she calls Tom to take you to the I hospital or clinic. Cheryl and Tom and my sponsors, may God reward you.

On one of those early days, the vice chairman of the area showed up. That area beyond the wall, with all its bushes and long grass needed to be cleaned up, he said to the Martins. It was theirs, it came with the house. For a couple of minutes, their spirits dropped as the implications of caring for yet more property sank in. Their own home needed attention. A dripping tap (important, when it is draining the water tank) had to be fixed. A lock had to be installed on the spout from the water tank to discourage water thieves. The garden had to be weeded and grass cut (slashed, in Uganda). And now, there was yet more property to maintain.

The bureaucracy. Tom had to pay the power bill, in person, at the utility company office. They are quick to cut off power, literally cutting the line. In a nod to customer relations, the office had a sign: "Inconviniences are highly regreted."

Feelings of irritation quickly faded, though, as the full implications of the chairman's statement sunk in. HCTH land holdings had just expanded. There was room for another house, and another garden, and more kids. Tom could hardly wait to tell the anonymous Canadian donor directly.

Conclusion

"SERVICE ABOVE SELF"

— Rotary International

Each year, Rotarians look around their community in search of someone who has made an outstanding contribution in the spirit of Paul Harris, founder of the international service club more than one hundred years ago. Sometimes, they do not recognize anyone, but, generally they can identify a worthy recipient. Only rarely are two chosen, and never before in Napanee.

In June 2015, two weeks after the tenth annual meeting of HCTH, the Rotary Club of Napanee honoured Tom and Cheryl Martin in recognition of their decade of charitable service. Each was named a Paul Harris Fellow, a Rotary International recognition of outstanding service.

In making the presentation, Rotarian Gilbert Myatt gave a capsule summary of their achievements, beginning with them raising more than a million dollars since 2005 for education, medical supplies, small business start-ups, and homes for orphans. Many children now were in school, and several in university.

"This is quite an amazing feat for two dedicated individuals," he said, reminding his audience that they pay all their own expenses. Tom and Cheryl were pleased by the recognition from their community leaders, but they see the award as a tribute to all of their three hundred plus supporters.

As they reflected on the growth and evolution of Helping Cope Through Hope, Tom says he finds the most remarkable part was to see how many people rallied around "two average retirees who felt they had a calling."

Except that it is a stretch to think of Tom and Cheryl as "average" because, by the time HCTH was born, they had already had a history of extraordinary service in community and church activities.

At the tenth anniversary annual meeting, Tom claimed that the treasurer's report "just blew my mind."

In its first year, HCTH raised $10,000. In 2014-15, the total was $188,000, and it's still growing. The generosity of supporters "of these average retirees" had exceeded their wildest dreams.

He pointed to the dramatic shift in support, where emphasis was now on helping students get into and through university. It was a shift they had not planned. It simply grew out of their recognition of the paramount importance of education. "We can't — and don't — say, when the children finish high school, 'so long, it was nice seeing you.'" For the second year in a row, he went to Uganda in 2015 to help students start or return to university.

Cheryl was more pensive as she reviewed the decade. She spoke about the joy of having people accompany them to the field; "You can almost see them connect with one child." Hope Angela, a Ugandan youngster adopted by two young people barely out of their teens themselves, jumped to mind. Being there "opens minds to missions."

Her enthusiasm is telling, given that those visitors add to her workload — she's the hostess, and often the chef, for the visitors. The burden of visitors pales against the value of their involvement, she says, adding that most visitors are willing helpers in the domestic activities. Most also use the opportunity to become personally engaged with children they sponsor or others with specific needs.

She focuses on the many successes, particularly on the newly acquired home for children in Uganda, a dream come true. Neither Cheryl nor Tom dwells on disappointments that they have encountered in their mission. Brief references in Tom's emails are the only glimpses of hoped-for goals that were missed. Most often it's students who, through either a lack of ability or interest, didn't achieve classroom results. Occasionally, it is adults who needed more hand-holding to take advantage of the opportunities presented to them.

These references lend a sense of reality to their work, but here's the thing: they do not criticize the individuals, nor is there a suggestion that failure brings abandonment. The opposite is often the case, where subsequent emails talk about their efforts to fix the problem.

The examples give veracity to their oft-repeated phase, "We love these people." It means that the teenager with the botched abortion is reassured with unconditional love. Or a new batch of chicks is bought for the individual who sold the flock without keeping a few for breeding stock.

Much can be summed up in this abbreviated account of one average day with Baven, a Zambian teenager. Tom begins by describing the heavy rain and his fifteen-minute bike ride, compared with Baven's forty-five-minute walk, to meet at Swan School. Tom with a rain coat, and she without. The issue was that she needed to pass six subjects in Grade Nine to enter Grade Ten. She passed five and missed the sixth by three marks and would have to repeat Grade Nine. Her mind was on other things when she took that test: Her mother had just died, four days after being stricken with yellow fever.

"She was disappointed about having to repeat, but resigned herself to that. I then went to the market to get her shoes, an umbrella, and uniform — all in the rain. She has a great attitude and will do well."

The optimism is, by any measure, a gift of being able to rise above the potholes to see only potential. In their own world, optimism is tempered with an acknowledgement that they are getting older, which raises two concerns. The first is that they are finding it stressful dividing themselves among three countries. Second is the undercurrent carried by the march of time. The Martins have no plans to retire, but they agree that, if they couldn't handle the many hours of travel, "it would be difficult [to continue]."

"We couldn't groom someone to take over. God would have to find someone...."

They shy away from the topic, while admitting that theirs is a unique set of circumstances not easily replicated. Their physical well-being makes travel easy. They can afford to pay their own bills. They have a diverse and growing support group. At the same time, they say that the future is in the hands of God.

Postscript

AND SO IT GOES

— Kurt Vonnegut, *Slaughterhouse-Five*

I found that in writing this story, the end kept turning into a mirage, always around the next corner. However, the account must end somewhere, even though the Martins' work does not. So it seems fitting to tell "one more story" as an arbitrary conclusion: a January, 2016 email. And, indeed, so it goes.

Dear friends and family:

I forgot to tell you that when we landed in Zambia it was 27 C. The days have been hot, but they need rain.

We are very busy. This morning, I left home at 7:20 a.m. to walk twenty minutes to the bank. I was the first one at the bank, which was good. On Saturday, I tried to use my bank card, but the machine kept the card and said the card was expired. We always are concerned that the money HCTH sent on Dec. 30 did not arrive. That has happened before BUT Praise God the money was there.

It is good, because I met Mutinta at eight thirty. She is leaving for her last year of university today and needed money. I am meeting Floribert at eleven for his university fee also. Last night, we met with our builder. He is calling later this morning. He is starting another house at the farm —Esperanza, plus building another goat pen.

Also yesterday we met with the man from Lusaka who is putting in a solar project for us. He is giving a quote of the cost today and will need to be paid. Also, we have decided to build a second fish pond. The first pond is doing very well. There are almost four thousand fish in it waiting to be harvested next week. There is a market for the fish...

After this, I need to buy bicycles for us to use here then give away when we leave.

... I forgot, I have to go back to the bank at nine thirty. I need to take out a large sum of money, and they had to get it ready for me. Thank you for your support, prayers and love.

God Bless each of you!

Author's Notes

The Martins' focus has not shifted during the eighteen months that I have followed them, reading and re-reading emails, attending their presentations, and talking to supporters. I feel that this account, even with its many short-comings, would not be complete without — as they say in some church circles — a "personal testimony".

When my wife, Penelope Williams suggested that "I write a book" based on the Martin experiences, I resisted. In recent years, I had periodically written articles for publication about them, and followed them with interest... but a book?

I had no idea that I would become so consumed with the project. More important, I had no idea of the transformation that would come about in my own thinking and expectations. The windows of my mind were thrown open, not just on church-driven charities, but a host of others — individuals, corporations, and governments — who really care about their fellows.

In preparing this account of the Martins, many questions and unknowns bubbled to the surface. Many are still unanswered, because a research project on charities was never the goal, and some of my nags persist. It is left to readers to reach their own judgments.

I learned so much about compassion, acceptance, and grace. I had walked the streets of Soweto, South Africa, and visited villages in Kenya, but never really saw the real underbelly of

African culture. We have travelled the world, but, for the most part, with blinders on. It was in Miriam's Peruvian home that I came face-to-face with deep-seated poverty, but that was also where hope really abounded.

Although I've long felt a kinship with Canada's native population, strengthened by the book *The Inconvenient Indian* and my personal experiences, my sense of responsibility as a citizen has become visceral. It is harder to be a bystander.

My work on this project introduced me to some wonderful authors who write about what either they or others are doing, people such as Nicholas D. Kristo and Sheryl WuDunn, who wrote about a host of people active in charities. Scott Harrison of Charity: Water was an inspiration. Jimmy Carter, who may have done far more for the betterment of the world since leaving office than he was able to do as president, and many others. Their writings awakened an interest that I had never known.

Subtly, my thinking has changed. In the Martins' world, there are successes and there are failures. Their enthusiasm and optimism never — at least outwardly — wavered. It is "we do what we can" and beyond that, the results are God's responsibility. There must be disappointment when a sustained effort doesn't pan out. But the Martins have epitomized what following the examples of Jesus means in day-to-day living. And, for the most part, without words.

Together with the HCTH supporters that I have met, this voyage has enriched me immeasurably. Fortunately, unlike this book, that enrichment doesn't have to end — if I am careful.

I became indebted to many while working on this project. The Martins were totally open, allowing me to read all of their files and spending hours in conversation. They were unflagging in answering my endless questions. They allowed me unrestricted access to their correspondence, their organization, and themselves. As a result, I gained a deep appreciation for their personal missionary style and the commitment of their supporters.

I am also grateful to these people who allowed me to interview them. Interestingly, they showed me the same kind of acceptance and trust that is so amply displayed in the work of HCTH itself. Thank you to all, and a special thanks to Matthew Fournier, the boy who came to Peru with his parents in 2014. Matthew, you make mighty fine chocolate chip cookies.

Errors within these pages are wholly mine.

I am indebted to my wife who was a constant source of encouragement, gentle critic, and not-so-gentle editor. As an author and lifelong editor, her task was a challenging one, since she had to carefully sustain "my voice" and protect the conclusions I drew. Her patience, coupled with her expertise, were — and are — valued beyond measure.

Finally, I had the whole-hearted support from the rest of our growing family: Gregory Allen Sackmann and Cindy Charters; Loranne Sackmann (my technology advisor) and Joe Fisher; Keith Sackmann; Matt Williams and Erinn Somerville, Sam Williams and Erin Cunningham. And then the little people: Patrick, Jacob, Joshua, Kristopher, Kieran, Ruby, Abram and Louis. And, finally, the little, little people: Mackenzie, Kayden, Bailey, and Isaak.

Printed in Canada